MARCO POLO

GRAN CANARIA

with Local Tips

The author's special recommendations are highlighted in yellow throughout this guide

There are five symbols to help you find your way around this guide:

Marco Polo's top recommendations – the best in each category

sites with a scenic view

places where the local people meet

places where young people get together

(100/A1)

pages and coordinates for the Road Atlas

North America:
Marco Polo North America
70 Bloor Street East
Oshawa, Ontario, Canada
(B) 905-436-2525

United Kingdom:
GeoCenter International Ltd
The Viables Centre
Harrow Way
Basingstoke, Hants RG22 4BJ

Cover photograph: Mauritius: Pigneter
Photos: Baumli (14, 20, 24, 36, 74); Kallabis (19, 43, 45, 51, 55, 59, 72); Lade: Jahns (32, 80), S. K. (28), Thompson (77); Mauritius: Feature Pix (52), Gierth (60), Hackenberg (12), Hubatka (99), Mollenhauer (90, 94), Pigneter (4), Schmied (56), Torino (23), Wenske (27); Schapowalow: Huber (8), Stephan (39); Touristik Marketing (11, 17, 70, 84); White Star (31)

3rd revised edition 2000

Author: Stefan Emmerich
Translator: Thomas Thornton
English edition 2000: Gaia Text
Editorial director: Ferdinand Ranft
Chief editor: Marion Zorn
Cartography for the Road Atlas: © Mairs Geographischer Verlag
Design and layout: Thienhaus/Wippermann
Printed in Germany

CONTENTS

Discover Gran Canaria!

Peaceful villages and lively towns, mysterious mountains and lush meadows, golden beaches and steep cliffs – an island of contrasts

'Buenos días! Hello! This garden is a surprise!'

'Sí, es muy bonito! Yes, it is very beautiful! Its attraction lies in its originality. Nothing here has been designed to look flashy or commercial!'

'May we look around?'

The guard at the gate bows and gestures with his right arm: 'Señoría, su casa! Ladies and gentlemen, please make yourselves at home!'

Only very few tourists cross the threshold of Gran Canaria's most beautiful country estate, the Finca de Osorio just outside the country road between Teror and Arucas, which lies some 300 metres behind the Dominican convent of Teror.

Teror is probably the most 'Canarian' of all towns on the Canary Islands. Its centre is the old town district, which is perfectly harmonious: picturesque little alleyways and cobbled streets, intimate, venerable squares and patrician houses, intricately carved wooden balconies and ornate window sills made by skilled stonemasons, a magnificent Baroque basilica and a path leading down the hill, which is lined with medium-size trees on both sides.

The dunes on the beach of Maspalomas reach up to 30 m in height

The scenery here in the country, in the centre sections of the island's north, where potatoes, corn, oranges, apples, pears and mangoes are cultivated on terraced fields, is reminiscent of the Rhone Valley and other parts of Europe, except that, here, you'll also see a solitary Canarian palm tree amidst a meadow of flowers or some huge century plants, and that the meadow is skirted by prickly-pear cacti. With each step a new vista opens up, including, 700 m above sea level, a magnificent view of the Atlantic Ocean foaming in the distance and of the urban chaos of Las Palmas at the north-eastern tip of the island. Gran Canaria's capital has a number of attractions in close proximity to each other: two volcano craters, an

History at a glance

c. 1100 BC
Phoenicians and Carthaginians discover the Canaries

AD 23–79
In his work *Naturalis Historia*, Pliny the Elder describes an archipelago, referring to one of the islands as 'Canaria'

1394–1460
Under Prince Henry the Navigator, the Portuguese sponsor numerous exploratory expeditions to Gran Canaria, but they all end in failure

24 June 1478
Juan Rejón, a captain serving under Queen Isabella of Spain, lands in the north of Gran Canaria with firearms and 650 men. The Canarians put up bitter resistance

29 April 1483
The very last of the Canarian resistance fighters capitulate, bowing to superior Spanish power

August 1492
Christopher Columbus stops off on Gran Canaria, leaving behind three nutshells on his departure

1670
The Dutch attack the islands but are successfully repelled

1797
The British admiral Viscount Horatio Nelson launches an attack on Tenerife and is seriously wounded. He signs a peace treaty with the Canarians and the Spanish

1852
Queen Isabella II declares the Canaries a free trade area

1888
The first steamboat postal service between the islands is established

1906
Alfonso XII is the first Spanish monarch ever to pay a visit to Gran Canaria

1927
The Canary Islands are divided into two provinces

1930
Gran Canaria's airport is built

Post-1945
With the increase in air traffic, tourism gradually develops

1975
Franco dies. King Juan Carlos takes over governmental responsibilities. Spain becomes a parliamentary democratic monarchy

1982
The Canary Islands achieve autonomous status. Madrid still exercises sovereign power over the archipelago

1986
Spain becomes a member of the European Union

1996
Record year for Canarian tourism: almost eight million travellers visit the islands

international port, lively streets with bustling stores, wide boulevards and sea-front promenades, exotic parks, an idyllic old town, imaginative residential areas, a fascinating ethnic mix of people, plus a marvellous beach that need not fear comparison with Rio de Janeiro's Copacabana. No city on the altogether seven Canarian islands has such vitality and *joie de vivre* as Las Palmas de Gran Canaria, home to more than half the island's 750,000 inhabitants.

Gran Canaria offers many surprises, pleasant as well as unpleasant. Its very name brings to mind images of an ideal holiday destination – it has become synonymous with swimming and sunbathing. Initially, it is a cliché that determines the way one envisages the island: a holiday paradise, where one lounges under rustling palm trees by the ocean and the sun shines on miles and miles of golden, sandy beaches. Not to worry: the popular cliché is true in many places, such as the centuries-old oasis by the lagoon in Maspalomas on the south coast.

Yet, Gran Canaria, the third-largest of the Canary Islands after Tenerife and Fuerteventura, has many more faces than one would imagine: next to inviting places there are also shady spots, and enticing places are juxtaposed with repulsive ones. Here you meet the old goatherd who gladly gives you a cup of fresh goat milk and would be embarrassed asking anything in return; there you find the cut-throat who charges you 500 ptas for a can of Coke and four dried-up figs. Here you are enraptured by the grand villas and chalets in Canarian colonial style; there you are horrified at the poor shanties and cottages made from debris and pieces of junk. In some areas these stark opposites come into view at a mere turn of your head. Yet, most of these contrasts on Gran Canaria are beyond 'good and evil', and they are precisely what make the island so interesting.

It is particularly the landscape that offers such unsuspected, varied and attractive views; some visitors have even claimed that it resembles three continents at the same time: Africa, Europe and America.

If you set out to explore the island's entire 1,532 sq km or to drive around it along the coast on twisting roads that, altogether, are some 250 km long, you might agree: the island is covered with meadows blanketed with flowers, romantic valleys and historic villages in the north; dunes that evoke the desert, endless stretches of sandy beach, modern tourist developments, exotic bays ideal for swimming and elegant marinas in the south and south-west; dense pinewoods, Alpine-like rock faces, glistening lakes and white-shining, remote mountain villages in the island's interior; and steep, rugged volcanic cliffs and mountain ridges in the west.

Within these main areas, there are numerous other landscapes. One day in a hire car is not nearly enough to discover all the island's hidden treasures.

Twenty-five major gorges cut deep into the island's surface. The number of minor gorges is about three times as large. Gran

Canaria's shape vaguely resembles that of a cartwheel, with its gorges, called *barrancos,* radiating like spokes from the centre towards the shore – even though actually only five of the large gorges originate near the highest peak, the *Pico del Pozo de las Nieves* (1,949 m).

Island of dreams or of nightmares? This is a question many people on their arrival here are bound to ask themselves, for the motorway leading from the airport to the south passes through a rather uninviting area. The box-like houses, their roughcast only half-finished, look tasteless and depressing; the abandoned tomato plantations, through which a fierce fall wind frequently sweeps, seem ghost-like and desolate; the garbage and dirt in some places give it a careless, slum-like look. Only some 200 km of water separate the steppe-like hills in the east of the island from the western tip of the Sahara Desert on the not so distant shores of the African continent.

It seems to be entrepreneurs who derive the greatest pleasure from this area. They know that their companies and businesses on both sides of the autopista skirt the eye of a needle through which more than one million va-

Modern resort complex in Puerto Rico

cationers from Northern and Central Europe pass every year, as well as many thousands of daily commuters: waiters, cooks, kitchen boys, plumbers, chambermaids, office workers, suppliers and delivery men, managers and construction workers.

'Costa Canaria' is the name of the magnet drawing them all here. Colourful signs bid visitors 'Bienvenido – Welcome – Willkommen'. The biggest surprise for newcomers to the island comes after an approximately 30 minutes' drive from the airport: on a hill, the four lanes of the highway afford a breathtaking view of Spain's second-largest single holiday resort after Benidorm, the Mediterranean Coast's New Miami. The famous El Dorado of vacations actually consists of several towns that have gradually merged together to form one sprawling resort. First comes Bahía Feliz, then San Agustín, Playa del Inglés, San Fernando, Campo International, Sun City, Maspalomas Oasis and Pasito Blanco. No one knows exactly how many beds in hotels and apartments are available for visitors. 150,000? 200,000? If one also counts the beds in the neighbouring town of Mogán a little further west, with its fishing and yacht harbours of Arguineguín, Puerto Rico and Puerto de Mogán, then the number is probably closer to 250,000.

In any case, there is no shortage of accommodation, and the same thing goes for eating, drinking, shopping and entertainment: the Costa Canaria alone offers at least 1,500 restaurants, taverns, bars, snack bars, discos, pubs and clubs, plus at least twice as many stores, shops, boutiques, supermarkets, car-hire companies, bureaux de change and real estate agencies. There is also an unusually wide selection of sporting and recreational activities. They range from a 'Wild West' town and a botanical garden and aviary to go-cart race tracks, swimming pools with water slides, miniature golf courses, tennis courts, a golf course, a riding school, windsurfing and sailing centres, to mock bull fights, Parisian cabaret Lido-style, live jazz, camel, donkey and jeep safaris, gambling casinos and amusement arcades.

That such a wide range of recreational opportunities can be found within just a few miles of shoreline is indeed quite remarkable. To be sure, it is not to everybody's taste, but those who have taken to its subtle charm, keep coming back year after year. Well-managed establishments have their regulars: up to 70 per cent of visitors have come previously or stay for an extended period.

Some visitors have also invested in property, even if it's only an apartment of no more than 35 sq m with a view of the ecumenical church in which masses are held, bible groups meet and concerts are given on a regular basis, all in different languages.

There are also English radio programmes, English newspapers, English food and beer. You need not worry about the language barrier, except if you want to break out of the circle of those tourists who restrict their stay on the island to bed, swimming pool, beach, shopping centre and disco. But even in the island's remote places the natives – who, incidentally, speak Spanish – have long since learned to communicate with foreign visitors.

The majority of tourists here are either English or German. Next come visitors from Scandinavia, who are said to have discovered this holiday mecca towards the end of the 1950s. Particularly the English have always had close links with the islands. As far back as 1595 Sir Francis Drake, in the service of Queen Elizabeth I, attacked Gran Canaria (on 7 October) in an attempt to plunder its riches. In the last century it was English pioneers who set up the first storage bins and silos in the harbour of Las Palmas. They introduced bananas to the island, developed tomato cultivation, founded the first banks, installed the first water and sewage systems and, finally, constructed the first power station.

Ethnically, the Canarians were originally Berbers. There are no longer any genuine original inhabitants on the islands, because almost all of them were extinguished or enslaved. The few survivors mixed with their Spanish conquerors and the island's immigrants from around the world. There can be no doubt that during the last 100 years the legion of merchants from India have left more of a genetic mark than did the original Canarian inhabitants.

These multicultural influences have made Canarians sociable and tolerant, to which is added a large amount of *joie de vivre* and a great sense of humour. While Canarians typically have a casual streak and take things in stride, they also work hard and can be proud of tremendous accomplishments. After all, within the last 40 years they developed an infrastructure that has catapulted the island into the 20th century. Today, sea water is treated in huge modern desalination plants. Quite many houses are already supplied with electricity generated from solar energy. In 1992, the Canarian archipelago became a full member of the European Union. For two years, the islanders have waited for a green light from Brussels for the Zona Especial de Canarias, a new tax shelter in Europe.

Fifteen years ago, the Canaries achieved political autonomy, which restored the islanders' feeling of independence and self-reliance for which they had longed for 500 years. Visitors sense this new-found self-confidence, the Canarians' vigour and their desire to move ahead. One can clearly tell how rapidly economic change has occurred by looking at the number of cars on the roads: today one in two islanders owns a car (by comparison, in 1960 it had been only one in twelve!).

The tremendous and steady growth has surprised the Canarians as well – and makes them somewhat proud, too. Although the Canaries were spared the ravages of both World Wars, their monocultures were destroyed several times, and trade and economic change came almost to a complete halt.

The Playa del Inglés with its beautiful dunes

Every so often poverty and food shortage became such a serious problem that thousands of Canary islanders immigrated to Latin America, particularly to Cuba – which at the time was still a Spanish island – and to the young republic of Venezuela.

The old ties across the Atlantic Ocean are still cultivated on many levels – in terms of family as well as cultural and economic connections. The high unemployment rate, which at 16.3 per cent in late 1997 had reached the lowest point in 15 years, is not the result of an economic crisis but of the high birth rate the islanders have had in the past. Contrary to the rest of Spain, it is still higher than the death rate, even though here, too, large families have meanwhile become the rare exception. The Catholic Church's moral code of the past is no longer as strict as it was only 20 years ago. The Church still plays an important role in island life, but it no longer dictates the way people lead their lives.

Foreigners moving to Gran Canaria and working there pose another problem to the job situation on the island.

You can get an idea of how seriously they take this threat to their livelihood by the number of newspaper articles and TV programmes that are dedicated to discussions about the educational system and to research. More than half the local government's annual budget of almost 507 billion pesetas is allocated to these two areas. Even the *Finca de Osorio* near Teror has been converted into an educational and training centre.

'On the Canary Islands, the latest greeting is: "Buenos días, Esperanza! – Hello, hope!"', someone who has been well acquainted with the island for many years recently observed. This certainly expresses a general attitude that even the weariest European in desperate need of a holiday finds stimulating and uplifting to hear. Who, after all, wants to spend their holiday amongst people who start their day with a listless 'Bonjour, Tristesse'!

Somewhat exhausted from our stroll in Osorio Park, we sit down on a bench behind the manor house. No matter where you look, there is not another soul to be seen. It is, after all, siesta time.

From architecture to vegetation

Some dracaena palms on Gran Canaria are several centuries old. An expert on the island will tell you all about this, as well as many other interesting facts

Ancient Canarians

We know for certain that Gran Canaria's original inhabitants were related to north Africa's Berbers. Their Stone-Age culture has left traces that are still visible today: caves, either formed naturally or cut in volcanic rock (tufa), served as living spaces and were used for food storage. Messages carved into rock faces resemble those of predynastic Egypt and bear witness to the beginnings of advanced civilization. This corresponds to the fact that ancient Canarians were not hunters or fishermen but farmers. They embalmed their dead like the Incas did, and the idols decorating their ceramics, half portly female beings, half mythical animals, were carefully executed and polished.

Even though the ancient Canarians, generally known as *guanchos*, had only stones, clubs and wooden javelins as weapons, in the 14th century they offered fierce resistance for decades to the conquerors who advanced with iron spears and firearms. Nonetheless, later on they found it easy to adapt, especially since they did not believe in demons and spirits but in one god, like their new masters.

It remains a mystery why the islands' inhabitants, whose ancestors after all had once arrived by crossing the ocean, no longer had any knowledge of shipbuilding and seafaring when the Europeans arrived in Gran Canaria.

Palm trees, bougainvillea, spurge and opuntia are typical of the island's vegetation

Architecture

All historic villages on the island are still graced with fine examples of traditional architecture. Only at the tourist centres are they rare.

The older Canarian country houses are Mediterranean in style; individual features can be traced back to ancient Greek and Roman times as well as to Egyptian and Babylonian architecture. This is true of almost all domestic

The Columbus House in Las Palmas today houses a library and a museum

buildings, from the basic *casa terrera* made of local unhewn stone, and usually consisting of just one or two rooms under a gabled, hipped or flat roof, to the many-storeyed town houses of the well-to-do middle-class citizens. The roofs of the old *casas canarias* often consist of rafters, with a network of small, hand-cut beams made of chestnut, which are supported by additional, thick wooden beams. On top is a layer of clay with reddish pantiles.

Particularly the two-storey houses of the wealthy citizens had a main entrance that led into a central courtyard. The traditional Canarian patio is similar in design and concept to the Roman atrium. The growth of the island's prosperity can be measured in terms of its architectural development through the centuries. In the years immediately following the Spanish Conquest, a number of churches were erected. Numerous buildings in the so-called Canarian-Gothic style were erected that often contained design elements prevalent during the Renaissance. They were the works of artists and architects from the Iberian Peninsula. During the 17th and 18th centuries, architecture on Gran Canaria underwent only minor changes. Apparently, Baroque and Rococo were not very popular. There are, however, still a few examples of these styles on the island.

The Canarians seemed to take much more to the stylistic elements of Neoclassicism. Up until the turn of the 19th century, it was mainly the Church that commissioned buildings. After 1830, its influence declined, due to the increased growth and power of the middle class. This second period of classical architecture lasted until approximately 1900. Particularly in Las Palmas, Art Nouveau flourished around the turn of the 20th century. Today, traditional buildings are juxtaposed with modern ones, which makes for interesting contrasts.

Beaches

The sea is tested for pollution every other week or so by the Canary Island Ministry of Health. If an unacceptable level of impurity is found, the sanitation system for the area in question is checked immediately. How seriously purity standards are taken is indicated by the fact that the European Union's blue flag for beaches with exceptional quality of water is flying not only on the beaches of Playa del Inglés and Maspalomas, but also on the Canteras beach in Las Palmas.

Climate

The 'Fortunate Isles' Virgil described owe their lovely climate – mild summers and moderate winters – mainly to the trade winds. These can shift, however, due to high and low pressure zones over the Atlantic Ocean, which is why, particularly in the summer, sometimes a hot, dusty wind from the east blows in from the Sahara Desert to the Canaries: the sirocco. Every blue moon the sirocco also brings locusts to the islands.

Occasionally visibility is reduced due to air, thick with sand and dust, from Africa. The Canarians call these climatic conditions *calima*.

In the winter, the trade winds move southwards. This can bring in cooler air from the west with cloud bursts. The second factor contributing to the Canaries' climate are the currents of the southern fringes of the Gulf Stream passing the islands. Here, it is considered a cold current, compared to its surroundings. Along the Norwegian coast, where the northern fringes of the Gulf Stream pass, it is considered warm. At any rate, in the Canaries it raises temperatures in the winter and lowers them in the summer, so the climate always tends to be relatively mild.

A keen observer once called Gran Canaria a 'continent in miniature'. He was certainly right. One would be hard put to find on the northern hemisphere so many climatic zones within such a small space as Gran Canaria. The northern slopes of the central mountain ranges have areas with far more than double the average rainfall of some regions in northern Europe. In January, the mountain peaks may be covered with snow – which is not surprising considering that they are between approximately 1,300 and 1,600 m above sea level – while down by the ocean it is a balmy 20°C during the day, and when, in August, with temperatures soaring to 42°C up on mountain peaks, the forest service's fire stations have to be on the alert, down at the beach, in the shade of a parasol, it is usually still a comfortable 25°C.

Not only are the trade winds a contributing factor to the temperate climate, they also bring about some spectacular natural phenomena. Watching clouds that have just passed over the mountains, for instance – clouds that only a few hundred metres before may have been so 'wet' that it began to rain – dissipate, float apart, evaporate and vanish is an unforgettable experience. Phenomena such as this can be clearly observed from almost any point high up in the mountains. The sky above is crystal clear, there is not a cloud to be seen towards the south and the sun shines above the ocean towards the west and the east, but above the northern part of the island is what seems to be a motionless cover of cumulus clouds, dazzling white or light grey and typically with crisp edges that resemble paper cut-outs.

Fauna

Despite its geographical proximity to the African continent, you needn't be afraid of savage lions, rhinos, poisonous snakes, spiders or scorpions. There simply aren't any. Contrary to the Mediterranean, there are hardly any mosquitoes either. The animal life on Gran Canaria is less varied than the plant life. You will find, however, many species of bird – wild turtle doves, Canary falcons, buzzards, indigenous crows, ravens, siskins, hoopoos, thrushels and, of course, seagulls, occasionally even ibises and wagtails. A variety of wading birds, such as the *correcaminos*, are pleasant company on the beach. The *capirote* sings beautifully with a voice like a flute, which has earned it the nickname 'Canary Nightingale'. Sometimes you can also spot the *palmero*, whose singing is more subtle. In the heathers and groves of remoter regions of the north and west, you can see and hear Canary finches – the wild ancestors of the world-famous canary birds.

Those who seek out rocks and walls can find various kinds of lizards, particularly the short-legged blindworms or, at night, geckos.

The most common mammals are stray cats and dogs. Attempts to curb their boundless propagation by way of sterilization has so far not had any lasting success.

Keen anglers will be interested to know that carp and shark can be found in the inland lakes. Butterfly-lovers should keep an eye out for the beautiful Canary Admiral, which looks different than its European counterpart.

Folk music and dance

If you are lucky, you may stumble into a *tenderete* on your travels through the island – a spontaneous local festival full of music and lively celebration.

The *seguidillas* are amongst the most popular songs, because their lyrics are invented by the singers as they go along.

Following an instrumental introduction, the singer will stand up and do his best to sing about what he is feeling or thinking at that moment in time. This solo describes in a romantic, funny or sarcastic way what is moving the singer – scenes are taken from everyday life and can cover themes as varied as love, eating and drinking, money, the lottery, work and lazing about, football or television.

Like the origins of folk music, those of Canarian folk dances are also quite interesting. The *isa*, for example, is a lively, exciting music and dance piece whose key constantly switches back and forth between major and minor. *Isa* is a word from the Asturian dialect, meaning *salta* – jump!

The Canarian polka originated in Europe, however, the Canarians influenced European music as well. The best example of this is the group dance *el canario*. Enslaved Canarians introduced it on the continent, where it became all the rage at high society balls. When dancing *el canario*, the dancers mark out the beat by slamming their heels loudly onto the dance floor. They approach their partners through a series of leaps, while their partners try to avoid them by jumping away. One variation of *el canario* is the *sirinoque*, also a very popular dance with quite erotic movements.

Traditional costumes and folklore are still part of life on Gran Canaria

Another popular traditional dance is the *folía*, which is characterized by its deep tone of melancholy and despair. It is reminiscent of the *bolero*, which originates from the Balearic Islands, and bears a resemblance to Andalusian music in its tragic overtones.

The traditional costumes worn on Gran Canaria are as colourful and varied as the music. Most villages have their own local dress as a matter of pride. Therefore there is no such thing as a national costume. On Gran Canaria, costumes are particularly cheerful and decorous.

Geology

The geological origins of the Canarian archipelago are still a matter of some academic dispute. According to one theory, the islands are solely the result of volcanic activity, without any connection to the continent. Another school of thought maintains that they are an offshoot of the African continent. Yet another theory holds that they represent the tips of a sunken land next to Africa or even the remnants of the sunken continent of Atlantis (Plato). The latest geological research shows that the truth lies somewhere in between the various theories. Some regions in Fuerteventura, for instance, were probably part of north-western Africa. Gran Canaria, on the other hand, is of purely volcanic origin. The wealth of volcanic rocks, traces and structures that can be examined here at the surface is unique indeed.

Local life

Canary islanders are known for their generosity, hospitality, sense of humour and tolerance. Yet, as elsewhere, they have limits, too. One should, for example, not plop down in local restaurants or churches quite as casually as one does at home on the rim of one's bathtub. Such behaviour irritates the locals, even though many Canarians have by now gotten used to seeing different kinds of 'civilized' Central Europeans. Despite these words of warning, in tourist centres near the beach, you can dine in a bikini or tanga; just as many Canarian women do so when they're on vacation.

All it takes to deal with Canarians is goodwill, the readiness to approach them and the willingness to discard preconceived notions. For instance, one should first ask the locals if it is all right to take pictures of them. While Canarians speak foreign languages only *mas o menos* (more or less), *un poco* (a little) or *ni un poco* (not at all), it is English in which they are typically most fluent, and you will be able to get across what you are trying to say. Whether you will immediately understand the Canarians, however, is questionable, as in rural areas the Canarian dialect is so strong that even continental Spaniards have difficulties understanding everything that is said.

The Canarians are very fond of children, sociable and have a strong sense of family on which, incidentally, they do depend when society at large fails them. Grandparents are often taken care of by their children and grandchildren. Finding a job or an apartment, making a business deal – many things are accomplished through family connections. An uncle, a brother-in-law, a nephew or a distant cousin, someone always knows the right people, the *amigos* in the right positions. Public life has a thoroughly human face. Whether in front of a window in a government office, at the cash register in a supermarket or at a bus stop – it can't get any easier to talk to people than when waiting in line.

Canary islanders are always ready to help, but you shouldn't necessarily expect things to happen very quickly and efficiently. Be advised to tune in to a different sense of time than back home. Canarian society runs things its own way. It doesn't work by someone pushing a button somewhere. The plazas, the village and town square, are an excellent mirror of the Canarian

The island's tasty bananas are important export items

soul. They constitute an animated stage for the theatre of everyday life. Particularly during the evening hours, they become lively and don't really quiet down until the late hours of the night and during siesta. Lunch 'hour' here lasts from 1 to 4 in the afternoon. The islanders keep to this religiously – perhaps because it is surely the best thing ever invented.

Vegetation

Gran Canaria is full of pleasant surprises for those with an interest in plants. Of the 1,700 plant species on the islands, around 500 are endemic to Gran Canaria – they can't be found anywhere else in the world. If you explore the island, you will notice that it has many different vegetation zones. The existence of such a wide variety of plant life is essentially due to the differences in altitude, climatic zones and regions that are facing the direction either from or towards which the wind is blowing. Characteristic plants here include spurge, which grows in huge colonies, and of course the Canary palm. Everywhere on the Canary islands you will find the opuntia cactus or prickly pear, along with species of agave and aloe. The wild 'dragon tree' is really not a tree but belongs to the lily family. It has become something of a rarity, though it can live for some 2,000 years. In the higher mountain ranges, there are the sturdy Canary pine and the laurisilva. About 30 varieties of the eucalyptus, which was introduced to Gran Canaria during the last century, now thrive on the island. Amongst the colourful ornamental plants that flourish here are the extravagant strelitzia, or bird-of-paradise flowers (the Canarians' secret heraldic flower), bougainvilleas and red poinsettias, which can grow up to 4 metres.

As in the Mediterranean, you will also find hibiscus, passion flowers and different kinds of narcissus. In short, the Canaries' flora includes plant families ranging from A to Z.

Canarian cuisine

Hearty stews, home-grown vegetables and plenty of fresh fish

One of the most common items on the traditional Canarian menu is any one of various kinds of *potaje*, a hearty stew that comes in a variety of guises. As in many southern countries, garlic and saffron are the most widely used spices.

Mojo, a cold sauce used as a zesty addition to liven up fish or meat, is a must in every Canarian restaurant. Sometimes it is poured over *papas arrugadas* – another classic dish made of small potatoes boiled, then generously sprinkled with rock salt and served in their skins. Yet another traditional staple of Canarian cooking, the origins of which can be traced all the way back to the ancient islanders, is *gofio*. This is a type of meal made from roasted grain (mainly wheat, corn or barley flour) and ground chickpeas, served either salted or sweetened. The latter are the basic ingredients of *ropa vieja*, one of the standard dishes, with various kinds of meat and thyme.

Amongst the exquisite delicacies on Gran Canaria are several kinds of fish – here, shark steak and papas arrugadas, which are boiled in salted water

The Canarians love to eat, especially in company – with family, friends or acquaintances – and mealtimes are lively social occasions that are never hurried. Between meals, *tapas* are very popular as snacks. These are bite-sized portions of regional dishes served at bar counters and *bodegas* as appetizers to go with your drink.

Canarian breakfast (*desayuno*) is usually not taken early but sometime before noon. It consists mainly of coffee and milk (*café con leche*) or a small strong espresso, either on its own (*café solo*) or with a dash of milk (*café cortado*), a sandwich or *bocadillo*, a white roll with sweet filling, such as jam or honey, or a thick wedge of ham, cheese or *chorizo*, the much-loved sausage spiced with hot peppers. Lunch (*almuerzo*) is usually eaten between 1 and 3 pm, and supper (*cena*) between 9 and 11 pm. As supper is served quite late, it's not unusual to have a late afternoon snack, usually a sandwich (*merienda*), to fill the gap. Lunch and supper are substantial meals that are served warm, but only one main meal a day has several courses.

Alcoholic beverages

Surprisingly, the most popular alcoholic drink in the Canaries is not wine, but beer (*cerveza*). The two main Canarian breweries are 'Tropical' in Gran Canaria and 'Dorada' in Tenerife. The quality of their beers is consistently high and the list of imported beers is endless. Whether Bud, Heineken or Warsteiner, no one goes thirsty for want of finding their favourite brand. (If you're used to drinking out of a pint glass or beer mug, then it may seem strange to sip your beer from the small Canarian glass known as a *caña* in which it is traditionally served.) After being neglected for centuries, particularly the wines of Lanzarote, Tenerife and La Palma are also becoming popular again. Various red wines from Tenerife, for instance *Viña Norte*, have earned the highest distinctions in France in the last several years. The *Bodega El Grifo* on Lanzarote produces excellent, albeit somewhat heavy, white wines.

Food

Not surprisingly, fish is a main feature of Canarian cuisine and you will find a wide variety of fresh fish of the highest quality that you would not be able to find back home. It is usually prepared in a simple and traditional way, either grilled or fried, allowing for the fresh taste to be fully appreciated. The daily catches of perch, bream, squid and all sorts of tuna fish are a real treat. Sole and shellfish, however, are mainly imported frozen from northern Spain and the coast of northern Africa.

Cooking methods

Many holidaymakers who dine outside the main tourist centres have difficulty understanding the various cooking methods. The main reason for this is that some restaurant chefs don't offer pre-prepared dishes, which are called *platos combinados*, but only the main ingredient, for instance, fresh fish. The waiter will present you with a number of different options so that you can choose exactly how you would like your food to be prepared.

The following list of culinary terms will be very useful:

a la brasa – charcoal grilled
a la cazuela – cooked in a casserole
a la canaria – Canarian style
a la plancha – fried on a flat iron pan with a dash of oil
a la vinagreta – marinated in wine vinegar
al ajillo – in garlic
al horno – baked in the oven
asado – roasted
ahumado – smoked
bien hecho – well done (meat)
cocinado – cooked
crudo – raw
en adobo – pickled or marinated
en salsa – with sauce
en salmorejo – in spicy sauce
empanado – with breadcrumb coating
frito – fried in a pan
flambeado – flambéed
guisado – braised, stewed
mechada – in white wine sauce, often with onions
medio hecho – medium (meat)
poco hecho – rare (meat)
relleno – stuffed

A café in San Telmo park

Restaurants

There are plenty of restaurants, bars and cafés on Gran Canaria to satisfy all tastes, expectations and budgets. You can enjoy any or all of the following national cuisines: Japanese, American, Chinese, Indian, German, Dutch, Scandinavian, English, Argentinian, Austrian, Swiss, Italian, Lebanese, French and Belgian, nouvelle cuisine and, not forgetting of course, Spanish and Canarian. However, Greek, Turkish and Central European specialities have yet to make their mark.

Although bread and butter are rarely mentioned on the menu, they are nevertheless included in the bill. To avoid any misunderstandings, it is often a good idea to quickly repeat what you have ordered to the waiter before he passes your order on to the kitchen. Restaurants are required by law to write out bills. The total amount includes service. Some restaurants calculate Canarian VAT (IGIC) separately at 4.5 per cent, but in some bills it is already included.

By law, restaurants are obliged to show their price list authorized by the Ministry of Tourism, and must provide a form (*hojas de reclamaciones*) on which complaints can be registered, if requested. You can fill in these forms in English and then send them to the Canarian Ministry of Tourism. In the past, this procedure has resulted in some restaurants being forced to close down when the cause for complaint was not rectified. The same procedure applies for complaints received about accommodation.

Restaurants are categorized using a fork system rather than a star system. The number of official forks (1–5) says little about the quality of the food, however, as only a few establishments actually apply for grading. In a five-fork restaurant, for instance, you may expect actual silverware and a bidet in the ladies' room.

The time for last call varies from region to region. Most restaurants close between 11 pm and 1 am.

Health food and vegetarian food

Health food is on limited offer on Gran Canaria, in pharmacies and in good supermarkets. Las Palmas has a number of health food stores (*centros dietéticos*). The best known is at Calle Perdomo 20, in the Triana district. They sell organic grains, seaweed, herbs, tea, etc., and also offer a small selection of vegetarian food.

Another recommended health-food store can be found in the south of the island, in the San Fernando shopping centre.

Arts and crafts

Shopping in Gran Canaria's markets and bazaars offers many surprises

Until quite recently, one of the main attractions for tourists in Gran Canaria was the fact that things were *'bueno, barato y bonito'* – of high quality, well-made and inexpensive. At one time, this saying could be applied to practically everything you could buy here. This is no longer the case. Especially for groceries, prices on Gran Canaria are generally the same as what you would expect to pay at home, and are often higher. Yet, on account of the weak peseta in 1995–96, things have become somewhat cheaper, despite the higher inflation rate compared to that of other countries or even the Spanish mainland. Prices also vary on the island itself. There is a difference between the prices in Las Palmas, and the surrounding regions of the north, and the holiday resorts which dominate the south, that is to say, between areas predominantly inhabited by local people and the more touristic centres.

Always an enjoyable experience: shopping at one of the weekly markets

Shops are generally open from 9 am to 1 pm. They then close for lunch followed by a siesta. The streets can be pretty deserted until the shops re-open at 4 pm, but they don't close again until 8 pm. Many department stores stay open on Saturday, and some are even open on Sunday, during the busy pre-Christmas season. There are a number of smaller shops selling daily essentials and leather goods, which have late closing times all year round, and are also open on Sundays and bank holidays.

Ceramics and pottery

Originally the *productos de cerámica* – plates, bowls, pots, mugs, jugs, storage containers and vases – were produced for everyday use in Canarian households.

Unglazed ceramic goods are produced in a whole range of interesting shapes and designs. There are plenty of so-called 'antique' pieces on sale. The majority of these are replicas of the island's ancient ceramic designs made using antiquing techniques. The decorative cracking and primitive paintwork all add to their charm. The clay used either comes from the north or is imported. At any rate, a very large number of these ceramic goods are handmade, without the use of a wheel, just as they always were.

Embroidery

The fine Canarian embroidery work known as *calado* enjoys a widespread reputation. Tablecloths and serviettes, blouses and shirts, aprons and bed linen are beautifully stitched with ornate and complicated patterns. The preferred fabrics are natural cotton and linen.

Much of the embroidery, or *bordado*, is brightly coloured, incorporating designs with still-life scenes, landscapes, flowers, people and animals. Those with a discerning eye will be able to detect the Venetian influence on Canarian embroidery. Fine fabrics imported from Venice clearly set the trend for *encaje*, the local lace. Vilaflor lace from Tenerife is particularly intricate.

Wickerwork

Wickerwork is called *trenzados* in Spanish. It is widely available on Gran Canaria. You can buy simple baskets (*cestas*) in all shapes and sizes, as well as brooms, mats, bags and the occasional lampshade. Local raw materials include cane (*caña*) or palm leaves (*hojas de palmera*). The *caña* birdhouses and cages are quite unusual and make original souvenirs.

Canarian knives

The island farmers (*campesinos*) still take their *cuchillos canarios* with them when they go to work in the fields or hunt for rabbits or pigeons. Canarian knives are remarkable not for their honed blades but for their handles, which feature an elaborately decorated inlay around the central steel section. Bone, goat or bull horn, silver and brass, ceramics and glass are the materials traditionally used in these intricate designs. The same patterns were also applied to Canarian table knives, but these are more difficult to find nowadays. It is far more common to see small replicas of the originals used as letter-openers or on keyrings.

Cigars

Although tobacco is grown only for domestic consumption, if at

The national lottery

Lottery tickets are sold on nearly every street-corner. Approximately one quarter of Spain's national income comes from Toto, Lotto and the other games of chance. Your hotel porter will show you the ropes if you want to try your luck. If you hit the jackpot and get the 'Gordo', the top cash prize worth up to millions (dollars and pounds!) you'll have difficulty taking your fortune out of the country. But you could easily just stay here!

More popular are the national lottery (Lotería Nacional, it's complicated), ONCE (played daily, very low pay-outs) and the Lotería Primitiva, whereby you have to get 6 numbers out of 49 to win.

A street in Puerto de Mogán in the south-western part of the island

all, conoisseurs throughout the world consider Canarian cigars, known as *puros*, to be superior in quality and taste even to the famous Havana cigars. It is, however, very difficult to get hold of Canarian cigars. With the increase in mass-produced goods to supply the tourist demand, the production of authentic handmade goods is in jeopardy. You will be successful in your search if you visit the arts-and-crafts shops of the Cabildo, e.g., at the tourist information office next to the huge centre or the *Pueblo Canario* in Las Palmas.

Markets

Many of the small towns and villages in the country have their own market day. These weekly, open-air *mercadillos* have plenty to offer visitors. The goods on sale range from fruit and vegetables, flowers, household items and cleaning products to jewellery, clothes and shoes, arts and crafts, gifts and assorted junk.

The main *mercadillos* on Gran Canaria are:

- Arguineguín (Tuesdays)
- Maspalomas and Vecindario (Wednesdays)
- Puerto de Mogán (Fridays)
- Maspalomas, San Mateo and Santa Brígida (Saturdays)
- Valsequillo, Teror, San Mateo, Santa Brígida and Moya (Sundays).

Covered markets are known as *mercados*. They are open daily from 7 am until 2 pm, except for Sundays and holidays. The range of goods on display is much the same as in the weekly markets, but, in addition, you can get fresh produce, such as meat, fish and seafood, various types of sausage and a selection of cheeses and other dairy products. The main *mercados* on Gran Canaria are:

- Maspalomas (San Fernando)
- Las Palmas: old town, near harbour (Mercado del Puerto) and Calle Galizia (Mercado Central)
- Arucas
- San Mateo

Celebrations around the clock

There is much laughter, singing and dancing at traditional Canarian fiestas

Anyone claiming that nothing happens on Gran Canaria isn't familiar with the *fiestas*, the traditional public festivals. Going to a *fiesta* could well be the highlight of your holiday. The islanders have an innate *joie de vivre*, which is expressed on these occasions in many ways. They are fun-filled, around the clock. The music is loud and lively, and people dance, sing, laugh, play, eat and drink... All of this takes place outdoors, under the open sky, on the famous plazas.

On a more serious note, the *actos religiosos* are solemn occasions, when masses and processions are held in honour and memory of a particular patron saint.

Canarian *fiestas* can last for several days and sometimes even weeks. If you wanted to, you could celebrate continuously for several months on end. As soon as one village has finished its celebrations, another one starts theirs.

The highlight of the carnival processions in February and March is the election of the carnival queen

Each area, town, district or parish holds at least one *fiesta* a year.

Most of them are held between May and September, with the high point being in summer when the fields lie fallow due to lack of rain.

If you want to know which festivals are being celebrated where, any hotel reception desk or taxi driver should be able to tell you. You will also see plenty of posters publicizing forthcoming festivals and there are a number of English-language publcations with listings available, which you can obtainatregular newspaper stands or shops.

PUBLIC HOLIDAYS

1 January: *Año Nuevo (New Year)*
6 January: *Los Reyes (Epiphany)*
19 March: *San José (St Joseph's Day)*
Maundy Thursday: *Jueves Santo*
Good Friday: *Viernes Santo*
1 May *Día del Trabajo (Labour Day)*
30 May: *Día de la Canarias (Canary Island Day)*
25 July: *Santiago (St James' Day)*
15 August: *Asunción (Assumption)*
12 October: *Día de la Hispanidad (Discovery of America)*

1 November: *Todos los Santos (All Saints Day)*
6 December: *Día de la Constitución (Constitution Day)*
8 December: *Inmaculada Concepción (Immaculate Conception)*
25 December: *Navidad (Christmas)*

FESTIVALS

January

★ Between January and March: *Fiestas del Almendro en Flor.* The beauty of the Almond Blossom Festival can best be seen in Tejeda and Valsequillo.

February/March

★ ⊛ *Carnaval.* Lavish carnival processions pass through the streets of Las Palmas in February and can still be seen in Maspalomas in March. Festivities reach a high point with the crowning of the Carnival Queen.

March/April

★ *Semana Santa* (Holy Week). The religious and spiritual high point of Easter week with numerous processions.

⚲ ⊛ 29 April: *Fiesta de Ansite.* Festival commemorating the final uprisings on Gran Canaria against the Spanish conquerors in 1483.

June

24 June: *El Día de San Juan.* Anniversary of the foundation of the town of Las Palmas.

July

⊛ ⚲ *Fiesta del Carmen.* This festival in honour of the patron saint of fishermen and seamen is celebrated in nearly every harbour. The high point of festivities is on 16 July.

August

★ *Fiesta La Bajada de las Ramas* in Agaete. The village celebrates

MARCO POLO SELECTION: FESTIVALS & EVENTS

1 Lucha Canaria
Canarian wrestling – a sport practised with religious fervour (page 31)

2 Carnaval
A spectacular carnival, on a par with Rio (page 30)

3 La Fiesta Mayor de Teror
The largest public festival on Gran Canaria in honour of the island's patron saint (page 31)

4 La Bajada de las Ramas
A lively and entertaining ritual festival invoking rain for a healthy harvest (page 30)

5 Almendro en Flor
A beautiful almond-blossom festival celebrating the arrival of spring (page 30)

6 Semana Santa
One of the highlights of Holy Week is the dramatic Good Friday procession (page 30)

7 Festival de Música de Canarias
Classical music performances of high calibre (page 31)

8 Football tournament
Even international teams compete in the Maspalomas annual tournament (page 31)

wildly for three days during this 'Festivity of Branches'.

September

★ 8 September: *Fiesta Mayor* in Teror. Ten-day festival in honour of the island's patron saint.

10 September: *Fiesta del Charco* in San Nicolás de Tolentino in honour of the village's patron saint.

October

☺ ✱ 6 October: *Fiesta de la Naval.* Celebrated in commemoration of the victory over Sir Francis Drake.

EVENTS

January/February

★ *Football tournament* in Maspalomas with international teams – an established event on the Gran Canarian sporting calendar.

★ *Festival de Música de Canarias.* Concerts are held in the theatre at Las Palmas throughout January and February, featuring many international orchestras, conductors and soloists.

March/April

Festival de Opera. The winter music festival is followed by an opera festival, which is held in March and April, also at Las Palmas.

★ *Lucha Canaria.* This is a form of wrestling that can be seen in numerous tournaments between February and November on Gran Canaria, particularly in the south of the island: in Arguineguín, Puerto de Mogán, Ingenio, Maspalomas and Agüimes.

Lucha Canaria was invented by the locals. Teams are made up of 12 men. Opponents fight each other barefoot in a ring. The one who first touches the ground when falling is the loser. The victor's team is then awarded one point and the loser is eliminated. The losing team is the one whose *luchadores* have all been eliminated. There are no special categories according to weight.

Lucha Canaria – wrestlers in the ring

Rally El Corte Inglés. Motor races – prelims for the European Championships – are held in various stages across the entire island. It is the biggest motoring event on the Canary Islands.

June

Festival Internacional de Música Popular. This folk festival is held in Las Palmas during the second half of June. It features performances from local and international folk groups in traditional costume.

November

Last Sunday of the month: *Atlantic Rally for Cruisers.* The yachts in this transatlantic regatta race from Las Palmas across the Atlantic, heading for the Caribbean.

December

31 December: *Carrera de San Silvestre.* This annual cross-country race starts at Playa de Inglés. Tourists of all ages are welcome to participate.

BAR
7UP

In and around bustling Las Palmas

Colossal waves crash against the cliffs of this spectacular northern coast

The north of Gran Canaria can be subdivided into the three distinct areas of *La Capital, La Costa* and *El Campo*: the busy capital city of Las Palmas; the coastline, stretching north-west of Las Palmas to Agaete; and the often verdant mountainous countryside around such places as Santa Brígida, San Mateo, Teror and Moya. *La Costa* is banana country.

Pavement café in Puerto de las Nieves

Hotel and restaurant prices

Hotels (H)
Category 1: from 20,000 ptas
Category 2: from 10,000 ptas
Category 3: under 10,000 ptas
Prices are for two people in a double room per night without breakfast

Guest houses (G)
Category 1: from 3,500 ptas
Category 2: under 3,500 ptas
Prices are for two people per night without breakfast

Apartments (A)
Category 1: from 10,000 ptas
Category 2: from 7,000 ptas
Category 3: under 7,000 ptas
Prices for a maximum of three people per night without breakfast

Bungalows (B)
Category 1: from 10,000 ptas
Category 2: from 7,000 ptas
Category 3: under 7,000 ptas
Prices are for a maximum of three persons per night without breakfast

Restaurants (R)
Category 1: from 5,000 ptas
Category 2: from 2,500 ptas
Category 3: under 2,500 ptas
Prices per person for an à la carte menu with three courses not including beverages

Important abbreviations

Avda (avenida)	avenue
ptas	pesetas
C/Calle/Carrer	street
No. (número)	number
s/n (sin número)	no number

Some of the plantations stretch for miles and miles until ending abruptly along the steep, rocky coastline. Often stiff breezes blow in from the ocean. Then, the massive, roaring waves, which can be as large as houses, make a spectacular and breath-taking sight as they crash against the cliffs, exploding into gleaming clouds of spray.

If you stroll through the plantation and farming villages, you sense history at every step. Some of the alleyways and middle-class houses radiate colonial prosperity; in between there are gorgeous buildings dating from before the Spanish Conquest, but also unattractively designed 'matchbox' houses built in modern times.

Going inland from the built-up coast, we reach *El Campo*. It is here that we find the traditional *casas terreras*, those basic, old farmsteads with their inner courtyards, patios and hipped roofs, surrounded by terraced fields supporting a mixed agricultural economy. The main crop cultivated here are potatoes, corn, watercress and various other vegetables, depending on the water supply.

AGAETE

(101/D3) This small unspoilt town with a population of 5,000, situated in the north-western corner of Gran Canaria, is one of the jewels of the island. A small road leads from Agaete down to the tiny fishing village of Puerto de las Nieves, where, sheltered by the new harbour wall and the old pier, the waters are still and crystal clear. The bay with its small black-sand and pebble beach is rarely crowded, even

MARCO POLO SELECTION: THE NORTH

1 El Valle de Agaete
No valley is more fertile than the valley of the watercress (page 36)

2 Sardina del Norte
Off the beaten track, you can discover some pretty and secluded beaches (page 48)

3 San Bartolomé de Fontanales
The laurel woods near Moya provide beautiful walking country (page 46)

4 Hotel Madrid
Friendly atmosephere in Las Palmas' old town (page 43)

5 El CAAM
The Atlantic Centre of Modern Art in the old town of Las Palmas brings together the traditional and the avant-garde (page 40)

6 From Cuasquías to Yurfa
Las Palmas' nightlife gets most exiciting on weekends (pages 43-44)

7 Rum-tasting at Arucas
Many a celebrity has come here for a rum-tasting session (page 37)

during the height of summer. A little way out to the sea, just off the coast, a rocky outcrop rises up some 30 m above the waves. This distinctive landmark is known as *El Dedo de Dios*, 'the finger of God'. A great deal of effort has been put into improving that area of the island. Most importantly, a marina and a lido on the beach with a sea-water pool and sunbathing area have been under construction for some time. The promenade already gives a fairly good idea of how the whole of this coastline will look a few years from now: like a miniature St Tropez, à la Canary Islands of course and near Tenerife.

The lights of Tenerife's capital, Santa Cruz, can be seen here at night. It only takes about two hours to reach Santa Cruz on one of the two car ferries operated by the Olsen line, owned by Fred Olsen from Norway. There are several daily departures from Puerto de las Nieves. Up-to-date information about departure times and tickets can be obtained from the port.

SIGHTS

Ermita de la Virgen de las Nieves

In this votive chapel, dedicated to 'Our Lady of the Snows', you can see the oldest painting of the island. It dates from the 16th century and is ascribed to Flamish painter Jan van Cleve.

El Huerto de las Flores

With its lush indigenous vegetables and its plants imported from the Caribbean, this garden is one of the most attractive on an island renowned for its varied plant life. The Garden of Eden must have looked something like this. The stately calabash tree's dry pods are used as rattles. As it happens with gardens on Gran Canaria, the plants keep growing, and today *El Huerto de las Flores* is no longer really a garden but more akin to a tropical jungle. It belongs to the community and is tended to by retired people. Admission is free. The entrance is only a few metres away from the church square in Agaete. *10 am–1 pm and 4–7 pm daily*

Lorenzo Godoy

At the entrance to Puerto de las Nieves, visitors are greeted by a monument of astonishing grace and elegance. This bronze statue depicts one of the town's most famous sons, Lorenzo Godoy, founder of the contemporary ballet company in Las Palmas.

RESTAURANTS

There are seafood restaurants clustered all around this 'snow port', directly by the ocean. Those who don't care for fish can go to one of the many *tapas* bars in town. You will also find a number of restaurants further inland in the Agaete Gorge.

SHOPPING

Casa Pello

A good crafts shop, especially for embroidery. *Plaza Tomás Morales*

HOTELS

There are approximately 400 private houses in the area offering bed-and-breakfast-style accommodation.

Casa Tecla
Three large apartments. *Opposite Casa Pello; Tel. 89 81 66; Category (A) 2/3*

Hotel Guayarmina
Basic cuisine, reasonable prices, 25 remodeled double rooms and two singles. Romantic and peaceful location, about 8 km from the centre of town. Swimming pool and bubbling mineral water spring. Ideal base for those planning to hike in the Tamadaba Forest. It used to be *the* hotel for honeymooners. *Los Berrazales s/n; Tel. 89 80 09; Fax 89 85 25; Category (H) 2/3*

ENTERTAINMENT

In the evenings, the main centre of activity is ☥ *in front of the church Inmaculada Concepción*

SURROUNDING AREA

Barranco de Agaete **(101/D3)**
★ The 10-km-long Agaete Gorge, the 'valley of watercress fields', is considered to be the most beautiful valley on the island. To reach it from town, follow the road signs to *Valle.* Yet, it is not only watercress that is cultivated here, the main ingredient of the *potaje de berros,* the popular Canarian *pot-au-feu.* The steep sides of the gorge rise as high as 1,000 m in some places, providing protection from the notorious trade winds. This results in a hothouse effect, ideal for the cultivation of crops as exotic and diverse as papayas and avocados, mangoes and almonds, bananas, but also tomatoes, lemons, peaches, apricots and even coffee beans.

At one end of the valley, there is a mule track that winds its way up through the tiny terraced fields of corn or potatoes, all the way to the top of the gorge.

The people inhabiting the valley live extremely modestly. Their life is not easy, but they would most likely not want to trade their dwellings with an apartment in town.

Some of the people there don't live in regular houses, but in caves that were cut into levels of rock that are not as hard as others. Three dozen families can easily live in these spacious caves.

ARUCAS

(102/C2) Gran Canaria's third largest town, with some 32,000 inhabitants, Arucas has a solid, respectable air about it – but unfortunately only the old centre of this capital of banana plantations. The other districts hardly have the appearance of urban, colonial

El dedo de Dios – 'The finger of God'

prosperity any longer. Quite a few of the houses here look somewhat run down and many areas are littered with building materials and rubbish.

SIGHTS

Cathedral

The neo-Gothic Cathedral of San Juan de Bautista (St John the Baptist) towers above the old town. The huge stained-glass window above the portal is particularly impressive.

Jardín de las Hespérides

This garden, which is part of the private park of the Margravine of Arucas, of the noble Massieu family, is an absolute must. The entrance to the garden is usually wide open. *10 am–6 pm Mon–Fri; Admission: 500 ptas (adults), 250 ptas (children)*

Parque Municipal

A stone's throw away from the Cathedral lies this small and elegantly landscaped park and botanical garden.

Rum distillery (Arehucas)

★ The rum distillery is open to the public and must not be missed. It is impossible to overlook: plastered on the imposing brickwork is the pre-Hispanic name of the town, Arehucas, which is also the name of the factory.

The *bodega*, or cellar, is a lively place where rum-tasting is conducted with a certain sense of ceremony. The plaques inscribed with the names of some of the famous people who have visited the distillery over the years are a nice touch. *10 am–2 pm Mon–Fri; Admission free*

RESTAURANT

El Mesón de la Montaña de Arucas

Near the rim of a volcano crater, this restaurant offers good, wholesome cuisine as well as grilled specialities. Amongst the excellent and large selection of wines are some quality, genuine Canarian wines (*Denominación de Origen*). Children's playground. 12 *noon–midnight; Tel. 60 14 75; Category 2/3*

SURROUNDING AREA

Firgas (102/B2)

About 4 km south of this farming village, with a population of about 5,500, lies the largest mineral water source on the island, which makes Firgas a sort of spa. Above the bridge that spans the Firgas Gorge, there is a magnificent ridge with sheer rock faces and rugged, romantic basalt cliffs. This ridge, which curves along for altogether 18 km on the road between Arucas and Moya, is ideal walking terrain if you're feeling energetic.

Montaña de Arucas (102/C2)

There is a sweeping view of the banana plantations surrounding Arucas from the top of the 412-m-high Montaña de Arucas. The route to the volcanic crater is well signposted and starts from behind the Cathedral.

GÁLDAR

(101/D-E2) The former capital of Gran Canaria (pop. 22,000) lies at the foot of *Ajódar* (*Pico de Gáldar*), a 434-m-high volcanic crater. Gáldar is rich in historic treasures. The following are amongst the culturally most significant.

SIGHTS

La Cueva Pintada
'The Painted Cave' is just one of many volcanic stone grottoes that were once clearly home to an ancient Canarian Royal Family. The wall paintings here, said to be 600 years old, were drawn with coloured pigments. In this respect, they are unique to the whole archipelago. *Cueva Pintada, Calle Audiencia de la Ciudad.* (Unfortunately, the caves are currently closed for restoration.)

El Drago
One of Gáldar's major attractions is the impressive dragon tree, planted in 1718, that stands in the hall patio (*ayuntamiento*).

La Pila
Almost as old as this Methuselah of island flora is the Baroque church of *Santiago de los Caballeros*, which stands in the leafy and picturesque town square. A number of ancient and valuable sacred objects are kept in the crypt. Ask the sexton or priest for permission to view them. Many children have been baptized at the green-glazed ceramic font (*pila verde*).

SURROUNDING AREA

Las Cuevas de las Cruces (101/D2)
The *Cuevas de las Cruces* are visible from the road between Gáldar and Agaete. They are frequently described by over-enthusiastic guides as the prehistoric dwellings of the original inhabitants of Gran Canaria. They are in fact gravel pits, which were in use during the construction of the road from Gáldar to Agaete at the turn of the century.

Reptilandia (101/D2)
More than 1,000 reptiles ranging from tiny turtles to fully grown boas and pythons live in this reptile farm on Mount Almagro between Gáldar and Agaete. You can also see the only bird-eating spider to be found on the island. The best time to visit is around midday, when the daily temperatures have reached their peak, because that is when the cold-blooded reptiles like to sit in full view soaking up the sunshine. *11 am–5.30 pm daily; Admission: 800 ptas (adults), 300 ptas (children ages 5–12); expert tours available for groups only; Tel. 55 12 69*

LAS PALMAS

(103/D-E1-3) Las Palmas, the capital city of Gran Canaria, is often described as the 'Rio de Janeiro of Europe', a slight exaggeration perhaps, but in many ways a justifiable comparison. The volcano on the nearby La Isleta Peninsula can be likened to Sugar Loaf mountain and the magnificent Canteras beach in Las Palmas bears a marked resemblance to Rio's Copacabana beach. However, the similarities end there. The exotic and hectic city of Las Palmas, with a population of over 400,000, is the largest in the Canarian archipelago and is much more cosmopolitan than any other Spanish city of comparable size. It is a working community with all the daily comings and goings, frantic dealings, with the progress, change and chaos this entails. Las Palmas does not really have one centre, but is made up of a number of neighbouring communities grouped together and stretching for sev-

Santa Ana Cathedral in the old town of Las Palmas

eral kilometres along the coast. The picturesque old town, known as Begueta (which means 'the tiny meadow'), is situated in the south of the city. It is here, at the mouth of the *Barranco de Guiniguada*, that the true heart of the *Villa Real de las Palmas*, the Royal City of Palms, is to be found.

Triana, the 'posh' part of town and centre of its southern side, lies beyond the Barranco. The main boulevard in this area, the *Calle Mayor de Triana*, has been made into a pedestrian zone.

SIGHTS

Canteras Promenade

The 4-km-long ✪ *Paseo de las Canteras* is popular amongst locals and visitors alike. While strolling along this promenade, or wandering through the nearby Parque Santa Catalina, you can meditate on whatever's on your mind, engage in conversation with a friend or simply relax to your heart's desire. Or perhaps you may simply want to observe the colourful world around you and even record it with a tape recorder or a video camera, as proof that this city is livelier and more vibrant than the static pictures in the tourist brochures indicate.

Everybody seems to congregate here – farmers and bankers, mountebanks and pickpockets. Hotels, guest houses, apartment blocks, restaurants, ice-cream parlours, shops and bars line the Paseo, acting as a kind of buffer protecting the pedestrians from the din of constant traffic, exhaust fumes spewed out by the cars and the noise from the discos and pubs, which doesn't stop until the wee hours of the morning.

Castillo de la Luz

This fortress was built in the late 16th century. Notorious pirates were blasted out of the sea by its powerful cannons. Today the fort houses a cultural centre.

Old town

The old part of town is surely the most idyllic quarter in Las Palmas. The grey basalt façade of the Cathedral of Santa Ana rises imposingly above it. It was built between 1500 and 1800 and is an amazing blend of Gothic, Baroque, Classical, Colonial and Canarian styles. The cathedral is currently being renovated, but the treasury has been left open to the public. *Tour of cathedral treasury: entrance at Calle Espíritu Santo; 10 am–5 pm Mon–Fri, 9 am–2 pm Sat; Admission: 300 ptas*

Parque Doramas

The *Parque Doramas*, the largest and most attractive park on the island, is a real oasis of peace and quiet – the perfect refuge from the general tumult of hectic city life. The Canarian village *Pueblo Canario* forms the park's centre. It comprises a concoction of towers, gates, courtyards and atria, as well as a café built in the traditional Canarian style. Folk music concerts are held here on *Thurs (around 5 pm)* and *Sun (around noon).*

Plaza Santa Ana

The lovely Plaza Santa Ana stretches out in front of the Cathedral. Here, one can find the old town hall, the dilapidated Bishops' Palace, a number of respectable middle-class houses, some bronze statues of dogs and hundreds of pigeons. It's difficult to tell where one building begins and another ends, or to make out whether the building you're looking at is a town house, a nobleman's palace, a ministry building or a museum in the midst of the narrow alleys and hidden courtyards that surround the square. The buildings all seem to interconnect and the intricate wooden balconies, one of their most salient features, seem to lead from one house to the next.

MUSEUMS

El CAAM

If you're under the impression that Canary Island culture starts and ends with ancient pottery, then a visit to this museum will make you think again. ★ CAAM, which stands for Centro Atlántico de Arte Moderno, the Atlantic Centre of Modern Art, is in the Calle de los Balcones, one of the loveliest streets in the old town, sandwiched between the Cathedral and the sea. Within just a few years CAAM has developed into one of the most important centres of modern art in all of Spain. New exhibitions every other month. *10 am–9 pm Tues–Sat; 10 am–2 pm Sun; Admission free*

Casa de Colón

The Casa de Colón (Columbus House) behind Santa Ana Cathedral is a magnificent example of early Canary Island architecture. The exquisite stonework and intricate carvings are evidence of their high level of craftsmanship. Nowadays, the building houses a foundation, a library, archives and a museum.

Paintings and sculptures on loan from the Prado in Madrid are exhibited on the second floor.

Exquisite examples of America's pre-Columbian cultures indicate the purpose of the foundation, which was established by the island's administration: conveying knowledge about America. *Casa de Colón; 9.30 am–5.30 pm Mon–Fri, 9 am–1 pm Sat; Admission free*

El Museo Canario

The Canary Island Museum in the old town is one of the most fascinating places to visit on Gran Canaria. Most of the finds from the various archaeological excavations on the island are housed here, covering the earliest periods of the island's history. There are models and reconstructions alongside anthropological collections, with a somewhat eerie collection of skulls and skeletons. The library (reading room only) is an important source of information on Canary Island history. *Corner of Dr Chil and R. Verneau streets; 10 am–5 pm Mon–Fri, 10 am–1 pm Sat, 10 am–2 pm Sun; Admission: 500 ptas; Biblioteca del Museo Canario, 10 am–8 pm Mon–Fri*

Museo Néstor

This small, highly interesting museum in the *Pueblo Canario* contains works that incorporate a wide range of vibrant colours, attesting to the artist's incredibly fertile imagination and sensual lust for life. Traces of Art Nouveau, Art Deco as well as Surrealist influences can be detected. On exhibit are representative samples of the oeuvre of Néstor Martín Fernández de la Torre (1887–1938), a superb artist with many talents. *Pueblo Canario; 10 am–1 pm, 4–8 pm Tues–Fri, 11 am–2 pm Sun; Tel. 24 51 35; Admission: 150 ptas*

Museo Pérez Galdos

Pérez Galdos, born in Las Palmas in 1843, was one of Spain's greatest writers. As one of the first Realist writers, he was on a par with Zola or Dostoyevsky. Today, his birthplace is a museum, whose magnificent inner courtyard indicates to the visitor that the often grey walls of the capital can hide unexpected green spots of great beauty. *C/Cano 6; 9 am–1 pm Mon–Sat; Admission free*

RESTAURANTS

La Barca

This popular restaurant offers freshly caught fish from the seas around the Canaries. It is a couple of kilometres outside of town, on the northern coast. *Bañaderos–San Andrés Carretera General del Norte, 2.5 km; Tel. 62 60 88; 12 noon–midnight daily; Category 2/3 (often very busy on weekends)*

Casa Montesdeoca

This restaurant is set in a romantic building that dates back to the time of the Inquisition. With its beautiful plant-filled inner courtyard, it is an oasis in the heart of the old town. Serves plain Spanish cuisine. *C/Montesdeoca 10; Tel. 33 34 66; 12.30–4 pm and 8 pm–midnight daily; Category 2/3*

El Herreño

Behind the Cathedral and next to the covered market, the Herreño has for 34 years been the best place to discover the entire spectrum of Canarian cuisine. The most reliable indicator of the quality of the food is that it is very busy and that there are always many locals amongst its customers. *C/Mendizábal; 10.30 am–1 pm daily; Tel. 31 05 13; Category 2/3*

El Novillo Precoz

Charcoal grill specialities from Argentina and Uruguay. Great, comfortable atmosphere. *C/ Portugal 9; Tel. 22 16 59; 12.30–4 pm and 8 pm–12.30 am; Category 2*

Rías Bajas

We recommend that you try shellfish and freshly caught fish. *C/Simón Bolívar 3, in Saba multistorey car park; Tel. 27 34 61; 1–4 pm and 8 pm–midnight Mon–Sat; Category 1/2*

Las Trébedes

Top-class restaurant serving creative and imaginative Spanish cuisine incorporating both traditional and modern ideas. Famed for its gastronomic weeks, during which the cuisines from each region on the Iberian Peninsula takes its turn in the spotlight. *Avda de Mesa y López 18, on the top floor of the El Corte Inglés department store; Tel. 27 26 00; 1–4.30 pm Mon–Sat; access for the disabled; Category 1*

SHOPPING

Artesanía

Tucked away in a little alley off Triana Street is a well-stocked handicraft shop selling authentic Canarian crafts. *Tienda de artesanía del Cabildo, C/Domingo J. Navarro 7*

Champaign and caviar

Especially during the winter months, a number of factory ships whose home port is Odessa or St Petersburg, but which are on a cruise in the West, make into harbour here. If you have hard currency (US dollars are best), you can move freely on board and feast on cheap caviar (about 4,000 ptas for two ounces or 56 grams) at the bar as well as purchase some very reasonably priced Russian goods.

El Corte Inglés

This department store (which has branches all over the Spanish mainland) on the busy Mesa y López shopping boulevard is the largest on the island. It stocks everything you would expect to find in department stores at home. The fashion departments take up by far the most space.

Flea market

A lively and popular flea market called ✪ *El Rastro* is held next to the Parque Santa Catalina every Sunday between 10 am and 2 pm. You can get all kinds of bric-a-brac and the jewellery, made from copper, plastic, leather, paste and ceramics, is awe-inspiring.

Triana

✪ This is one of the liveliest shopping areas in the city and it's only a two-minute walk from the central bus station. It is centred around a well laid-out pedestrian zone, with tubs full of plants and flowers, and plenty of benches on which to rest your weary feet. A great place for window-shopping.

HOTELS

There are hundreds of hotels, guest houses and apartment buildings in Las Palmas. This is only a small representative selection.

Hostal Perojo

Seventeen basic double rooms, with a bathroom on each floor, and centrally located (near the bus terminal). *C/Perojo 1; Tel. 37 13 8; Category (G) 1*

This historic landmark is the seat of the distinguished Gabinete Literario club

Hotel Madrid

★ The only hotel in the old town. Popular amongst students, good, plain food, great terrace bar, 25 old double rooms with friendly atmosphere. Illustrious visitors, such as Dalí and Gregory Peck, have stayed here. *Plaza Cairasco 4; Tel. 36 06 64; Fax 38 21 76; Category (H) 2/3*

Hotel-Pension Plaza

Popular amongst young people. Forty-five clean, basic double rooms with a view of the Parque Santa Catalina. However, not the quietest of places, with a red-light district just around the corner. *C/Luis Morote 16; Tel. 26 52 12; Category (G) 2*

Hotel Reina Isabel

On the Canteras beach. Roof-top swimming pool. Terrace café with sea view. Restaurant/grill. 226 basic but comfortable double rooms. *Paseo de las Canteras; Tel. 26 01 00; Fax 27 45 58; Category (H) 3*

Hotel Santa Catalina

The best and most expensive hotel in the city. In-house casino. 208 stylish double rooms, quiet location. There is a good restaurant, *Las Casitas*, just around the corner. *Parque Doramas; Tel. 24 30 40; Fax 24 27 64; Category (H) 1*

ENTERTAINMENT

★ The variety of Las Palmas' nightlife is impressive. There are different centres for different kinds of entertainment. Around the Parque Santa Catalina, you'll find typical harbour life, but it gets more respectable as you approach the sea promenade.

Cuasquías

Jazz in a magnificent inner courtyard. *C/San Pedro 2; 10.30 pm–2.30 am Mon–Sat*

Destilería

Art is exhibited here and even the bar is an exhibit piece in itself. *C/Perdomo 20; 10.30 pm–4 am Mon–Sat*

Donosti

Amongst the regular bars in the beach area, doubtless one of the best. *Paseo de las Canteras 41; 10 pm–1.30 am Wed–Mon; Tel. 27 67 16*

Off Shore

Terrace bar directly above the cliffs, for surfers as well as web surfers. Nice furniture and fast-food quality. *Plaza de la Puntilla s/n; 12 noon–2 am daily; Tel. 46 15 55*

Le Pequeña Habana
Small salsa club on the lively Plazoleta Farray. *C/Fernando Guanarteme 45; 11 pm–3.30 am Mon–Sat*

Rock Café
Rock music and exquisite beers near the equally 'rocky' Plaza de España. *Mesa y López 35; 6 pm–3.30 am daily; Tel. 909 12 68 80*

Wilson
The audience in the *Discoteca Wilson* is mixed, but the music more middle-of-the-road. *C/Franchy y Roca 20; from 11 pm*

Yurfa
Art, drinks and beverages in a patrician house. *C/Perdomo 26; 10.30 pm–3.30 am daily*

BEACHES

The yellow-brownish sandy beach betwen Las Palmas and Las Canteras is about 3 km long and up to 100 m wide. It is kept fairly clean, but is very crowded, especially in the summer and on weekends. A barrier made of rocks (*La Barra*) at about 200 m from the edge of the water protects it from high breakers and allows you to go swimming even when the sea is rough.

Playa de las Alcaravaneras
This sandy beach on the north-east side of the city by the harbour is about 350 m long and up to 50 m wide in places. Suitable for sunbathing only.

Playa de la Laja
Darkish brown sandy beach with rocky patches in places, to the south of the city, right next to the motorway. The water isn't all that clean. Even though the sea is often rough, this beach is very popular amongst the locals.

INFORMATION

Tourist Information Office – Casa del Turismo
Parque Santa Catalina, 9 am–12 noon Mon–Fri; Tel. 26 46 23

SURROUNDING AREA

Jardín Botánico (103/D3–4)
Gran Canaria's Botanical Garden, the *Jardín Botánico Viera y Clavijo*, is near Tafira, about 7 km above (and south-west of) Las Palmas on the Carretera del Centro, the main road leading to the mountains. You don't have to take a keen interest in botany to appreciate this garden. How-

Royal roads

Walking, hiking and mountain-biking through gorges, forests and fertile valleys, called *turismo rural*, rural tourism, is so popular amongst the Canarians that the island's government has turned its attention to the long-neglected *caminos reales* and has lately issued maps of these old goatherds' paths (C/Cano 25, 10 am–1 pm and 5–8 pm Mon–Sat; Tel. 38 15 39). You can obtain information on mountain guides and accommodation in the country and mountains by contacting the Patronato de Turismo in Las Palmas (C/ Bravo Murillo 13; 9 am–1.30 pm Mon–Fri; Tel. 38 39 55).

The caves of El Cenobio de Valerón once served as a storehouse

ever, do not expect to see a profusion of flowers in bloom, for there is no artificial garden landscaping here. The flora and fauna are displayed in their natural settings – flat plains, sloping fields and rocky terrain. Everything is grown respecting the natural contours of the land. This 150-acre parkland is more like a nature reserve than a formal garden.

There is a great view of the whole garden from the *Jardín Botánico*, which is modelled on a typical Canary island farmhouse. Simple but tasty food. *Tel. 35 16 45; 12 noon–4 pm and 8–11 pm daily; Category 2/3*

Botanical Garden 8 am–6 pm daily; Admission free

MOYA

(**102/B2**) This small-town farming community with a population of 8,000 lies on a rocky plateau between Gáldar and Arucas, in the foothills of the central massif.

SIGHTS

Parish church

The parish church stands in solitary splendour above the rugged *Barranco de Moya*, whose top region is called *Barranco de los Tilos*: gorge of the linden trees. However, there really are no linden trees – and never have been – but instead *Tiles*. These are Canarian laurel trees. Signs are clearly posted along C 814 between Moya and Guía.

From the square in front of it, you get a fantastic view of the fertile *barranco* and of the Atlantic Ocean in the distance. Turning to the church itself, the columns on the portals are remarkable, each one made from a single piece of basalt. They are a fine example of the almost extinct art of stonemasonry.

MUSEUM

Museo Casa Morales

Near the church is the charming little Morales Museum, which is dedicated to the life and work of the Canarian poet and doctor Tomás Morales (1886–1921). *Calle Miguel Hernández; Tel. 62 00 02; normally 10 am–2 pm Mon–Fri (by appointment only); Admission free*

HOTEL & RESTAURANT

El Cortijo
A lovely hotel/restaurant tucked away in the hills. Ideal for romantics. Five comfortable double rooms. A little cool in the winter. Interesting menu. *Carretera Moya-Fontanales, 21.3 km; Tel. and Fax 61 02 85; Category (H) 3, (R) 2*

SURROUNDING AREA

San Bartolomé de Fontanales (102/A4)
The island's 'rain centre' is near the sleepy little village of San Bartolomé de Fontanales, above Moya. Even on your way there, you will easily believe that average annual precipitation in this area can be up to 1,000 litres of rain per square metre. On both sides of the winding road you see green, green, and still more green, as far as the eye can see. ★ Here you can get a wonderful impression of what the entire island must have looked like in the old days. The laurel forest used to stretch all the way down to the lower regions.

SANTA BRÍGIDA

(102/C4) The Carretera del Centro takes you up into Santa Brígida, just 15 km outside Las Palmas. The appearance of this neat and prosperous little town is a bit of a shock to the system after the dusty and barren areas around Las Palmas. It is surrounded by swaying cypress trees and all sorts of conifers, as well as exotic date and Canary palms. In some places there is so much greenery and such a crush of flowers in so many different, beautiful colours, that it's hard to decide where to look first. This is one of the wealthiest suburbs of Las Palmas.

RESTAURANTS

Las Grutas de Artiles
Stunningly beautiful location, off the street leading to the lush and verdant Angostura Valley, with caves and tables under deciduous trees. In the summer, live music and dancing every weekend. Gorgeous design complete with caves, tropical plants, a swimming pool and tennis courts. *11 pm–1 am daily, Saturdays dancing until 3 am; Santa Brígida, C/ Las Meleguinas s/n (a little off the beaten track); Tel. 64 05 75 or 64 12 50; Category 2/3*

El Martell
The road from Santa Brígida to San Mateo twists and turns through fields, meadows and small patches of woodland. You'll pass many tiny villages along the way, places like Portada Verde, Gran Parada and El Madroñal, all of which have good restaurants. The most 'typical' of them all is bound to be *El Martell*. This establishment, with its authentic rural décor, sells the best red wine on the island. It is stored on the premises in huge wooden casks and you can ask for a few bottles to be filled for you to take away, but be prepared to pay for it – quality doesn't come

cheaply. Wine buffs swear by the dry table wine known as Vino del Monte. Apparently, even Shakespeare was an avid fan of Canary Island wine – in his time, a large part of the island was covered by vineyards. Unfortunately, around the middle of the 19th century, a plague of phylloxera (an insect that feeds on vines) and mildew resulted in a sharp decline in the wine trade. Today, viticulture is on a small scale and production is mainly concentrated in the region between Santa Brígida and Tafira. A quality Malmsey (Malfasia) is still produced here, which owes its distinct taste to the volcanic soil and climate. *El Madroñal, Carretera del Centro, 200; Tel. 64 12 83; 12 noon–5 pm and 8 pm–midnight daily; Category 2*

SURROUNDING AREA

(102/C4) You can take wonderful strolls and walks from Santa Brígida into the Angostura Valley.

SANTA MARÍA DE GUÍA

(101/E2) The Carretera del Norte, the four-lane highway from Las Palmas to the northwest corner of the island, comes to an end at Santa Guía, known to the locals simply as Guía. This means that through-traffic often gets conjested in the town and a clear run is really only possible during siesta time. So rather than sit in a traffic jam for hours trying to make it through the town, get out and have a look around the old 'banana capital' with its population of 14,000.

SIGHTS

Old town

The heart of the town, *El Casco Urbano*, has a touch of patrician noblesse – cobbled streets and imposing houses featuring carved wooden portals. The statue of the Virgin Mary in the parish church, which stands in an impressive square, was sculpted by Lujan Pérez (1756–1815). Born in Guía, he was one of the foremost sculptors and artists of the Canary Islands. Many examples of his work can be seen in churches scattered throughout the islands.

SHOPPING

Los Quesos

This curious shop owned by Don Arturo Díaz Godoy (right on the main road, near the Texaco gas station) is crammed with cheese of every description and deserves more than a cursory visit. The shop stocks every type of sheep and goat's cheese imaginable, and alongside all the cheese and *tapas* on offer, you can find all sorts of farming objects from handmade banana knives and woven baskets to ceramic pots and goat bells.

You simply must sample the Canarian country honey, *miel del país*, which goes well with a drop of *Ron de Aldea*, a rare specimen of the island's rums, while the *Vinito Moscatel* (muscatel wine) is a perfect complement to the local aromatic cheese, *queso del flor*, which is made with artichoke flowers. There is also a good selection of handmade souvenirs and kitchen utensils. *Carretera General, Lomo de Guillén 17; 9 am–2 pm and 4–9 pm Mon–Fri, 9 am–3 pm Sat and Sun*

SURROUNDING AREA

El Cenobio de Valerón **(101/E2)**
One of the main tourist attractions of the island is the ancient ✳ *Cenobio de Valerón* in the Silva Gorge just north of Guía. It probably served the original islanders as a storehouse. The whole complex is made up of approximately 350 rooms, which were either adapted from the existing formations or hewn from the soft volcanic rock. The rock face provided protection from attack. *10 am–1 pm and 3–5 pm Mon–Sat*

San Felipe **(102/B2)**
It is well worth making a detour to visit one of the tiny farming villages which can be found between Guía and Bañaderos. San Felipe is particularly worth visiting as it boasts two magnificent rocky beaches, where you can sit and watch the local fishermen landing their catch with agility and bravura. Rod in hand, they clamber over the slippery, razor-sharp basalt rocks as the sea crashes around them, sending great clouds of spray that threaten to engulf them.

SARDINA DEL NORTE

(101/D1-2) ★ This coastal village lies about 6 km west of Gáldar. It does not have much to offer the tourist at first sight, but it is a quite popular place for left-wing pilgrims of Gran Canaria who come here to commemorate the huge demonstrations that took place during Franco's regime. At that time the village became famous as news of the locals' bravery spread.

RESTAURANT

La Fragata
At the end of the sea promenade is this excellent restaurant, where Jean Paul prepares your food according to the culinary standards of his French homeland. *Playa de Sardina; 11.30 am–11 pm Tues–Thurs; Tel. 88 32 96; Category 2*

BEACHES

★ The lower part of Sardina del Norte is the most idyllic. The water in the tiny bay nestling between volcanic cliffs is mostly crystal clear and the fine sandy beach is about 50 m long. Since it's quite an out-of-the-way place, only a few tourists choose to come here and so the beach is never very crowded.

There are a number of other beaches along the coastal stretch between Sardina and Gáldar, but most of them are rocky. One of the best is the Bocabarranco Beach, which many people are not familiar with. If it were in the island's south, it would surely not be so unkempt. With its deserted promenade, empty run-down houses and scruffy sea-water pool, the whole place feels a bit like a ghost town. Not far from here is *La Necrópolis*, a fenced-in cemetery for original islanders that has tumble-down burial chambers.

TAFIRA

(103/D3-4) The most attractive suburb of Las Palmas is only five minutes by car from *Vegueta*, the city's old town. It straddles both sides of the *Carretera del Centro* and rises to heights of 300 to 400 m.

The whole district incorporates Tafira Baja (Lower Tafira), Monte Coello, Monte Lentiscal (Mid-Tafira) and Tafira Alta (Upper Tafira).

These are the rich suburbs of Las Palmas, where the more privileged citizens live in sumptuous villas with beautifully tended gardens. Tafira has always been popular amongst the wealthy islanders. An increasing number of professional or retired Spanish, English and Germans are making this area their home.

The people living there are somewhat taken by surprise when asked about the history of their noble neighbourhood. Their explanations usually don't tell the whole truth, which is that everyone has always wanted to live more extravagantly than their neighbours. The range of styles amongst these 'façades of power' is remarkable: everything is represented, from Doric pillars and the ostentatious Baroque to the more stark and modern styles of Bauhaus and Le Corbusier. Many of the 'miniature palaces' exude the quiet and meditative atmosphere. The most charming residences in this neighbourhood are those that are somewhat run down, recalling the days of old.

SIGHTS

Pico de Bandama

Any visit to Tafira should include an excursion to ⁂ *Pico de Bandama* (574 m). The approach to this impressive volcano is well signposted from the main road and the view from the top of the crater is simply breathtaking. The whole of the northern part of the island stretches out before you, and, on a clear day, Fuerteventura can be seen in the distance. The volcanic ash deposited in layers of varying thickness around its slopes contains natural properties that are very beneficial to farmers. The porous, black 'crumbs', known to geologists as lapilli and to the islanders as *picón*, are hygroscopic: they readily absorb moisture from the atmosphere and conduct it down to the soil below. This 'dry-field' method of irrigation is also widely used in hotel gardens.

RESTAURANT

Satautey

Restaurant run by the College of Hotel Management. Excellent cuisine, formal atmosphere. *C/Real de Coello 2; 2–4 pm and 7.30–11 pm daily; Category 1/2*

SPORTS & LEISURE

Bandama Golf Club

This picturesque golf course is laid out on the south side of the crater. The rough has been planted with a wide variety of flora endemic to the island and is more like a botanical garden than a golf course. The Bandama Golf Club, founded in 1891 by British residents, is the oldest in Spain. The 18-hole course is over 5.5 km long and is quite hilly, with a height differential of 40 m.

HOTEL

Hotel Golf Bandama

Informal hotel with 27 double rooms and 12 singles, all with private bathrooms. Terrace, swimming pool, tennis courts and riding stables. Golf, tennis and riding lessons are available; please inquire. *Tel. 35 33 54; Fax 35 12 90; Category (H) 2*

SURROUNDING AREA

La Atalaya **(103/D4)**
There are a number of hill-top villages on the island whose names include the word 'atalaya', which means 'look-out' or 'watchtower'. The most famous of these hill-top settlements is La Atalaya de Santa Brígida, which lies to the south-west of Tafira, 500 m above sea level. The elevated position of villages like this was very important in ancient times, as it meant that advance warning could be given of visitors approaching the island from the sea.

It isn't obvious at first glance that Atalaya is really a cave-village because most of the original cave dwellings now have houses built in front of them. From earliest times, Atalaya was renowned for its ceramics, such as jugs, pots and bowls, which today are produced almost exclusively by old people.

TEROR

(102/B-C3-4) There is no place on the entire island that has become the subject of as many folksongs and poems as Teror. They are all evergreens of island folklore: songs about the pilgrimage to Teror, the town itself, the nearby spring and hymns to the Virgen del Pino (Madonna of the Pine), patron saint of the island, whose basilica forms the heart of the community (pop. 14,000). Officially Teror is 'Villa Mariana', a market place in commemoration of the Virgin Mary – a distinction that expresses Teror's religious significance as a pilgrimage site, to which the town's beautiful basilica points as well.

SIGHTS

Nuestra Señora del Pino
The basilica in its present form dates from the 18th century and is one of the most impressive churches on the island. There is a golden altar and a chamber dedicated to the Madonna's image. *Open all day*

MUSEUMS & GALLERIES

Don Jorge Art Gallery
The studio of the German artist Georg Hedrich, more familiarly known as Don Jorge, is directly opposite the basilica. *Tel. 63 17 16; 11 am–5 pm Tues–Thurs*

Museo Manrique de Lara y Bravo de Laguna
This museum, dedicated to life on Gran Canaria, is in a 300-year-old building on the main square. The magnificent gallery around the fountain patio is made of 'tea', the reddish heartwood of the Canary pine. Well worth a visit. *Plaza Nuestra Señora del Pino 3; 11 am–6 pm Mon–Sat, 11 am–2 pm Sun; Admission: 300 ptas*

SURROUNDING AREA

Valleseco **(102/B4)**
A delightful road lined with eucalyptus trees winds its way from Teror up to the largely unspoilt farming village of Valleseco 8 km from Teror and 950 m above sea level. At the heart of the village stands a lovely church with a striking white Moorish roof. Valle-

seco actually means 'dry valley', which is rather ironic considering that it is in one of the wettest areas of Gran Canaria. Water gushes through the *acequías* (irrigation channels), which carry it down to the banana plantations of Arucas. Potatoes are the main crop cultivated in the fertile fields around the village, but there are also a few orchards and vegetable plots. Time seems to have stood still here and it's not uncommon to see a *campesino*, a local farmer, loading up his donkey with feed for his cattle in time-honoured fashion.

Like the neighbouring village of Lanzarote, Valleseco is an ideal base for exploring the surrounding countryside, whose fields are crossed with footpaths and trails.

The pilgrimage town of Teror is Gran Canaria's most important religious centre

VEGA DE SAN MATEO

(102/C5) The neat and tidy fields of cereal crops and the rich green meadows that blanket the area are reminiscent of a landscape in southern Germany. The 'meadow of St Matthew', as the name of the town with a population of 8,500 translates, is at a point 650 m above sea level where the *Carretera del Centro*, the main road between Las Palmas and Cruz de Tejeda, and the country road between Telde and Teror cross. Oranges and lemons are cultivated here at altitudes up to 1,000 m.

MUSEUM

La Casa de Cho Zacarías
This privately run ethnological museum has a wonderful display of agricultural equipment and other domestic implements that were commonly used on Gran Canaria in centuries past. It gives a real insight into the rural life of Gran Canaria. *Daily except Sun, 10 am–1 pm; Admission: 400 ptas.* A restaurant of the same name is attached to the museum.

RESTAURANT

La Casa de Cho Zacarías
As select as everything else in *La Casa de Cho Zacarías*, the lunch menu offers the very best in Canarian cuisine. Sometimes (usually when there is a coach party) folk music is played while you eat. *Carretera General (main street); 1–4 pm daily except Mon; Tel. 66 06 27; Category 2/3*

SURROUNDING AREA

Las Lagunetas (102/B5)
The charming hamlet of Las Lagunetas (situated between San Mateo and Cruz de Tejeda) is the highest settlement in the beautiful Valley of Guiniguada, whose mouth is in Las Palmas, between the market and the theatre.

Mountains and volcanoes

An undisturbed haven waiting to be explored

Canarians refer to the interior mountainous region of the island as the *cumbre*. This is Spanish for mountain peak and technically stands for anything higher than 10,000 m. This central mountain massif provides a fabulous landscape, but is difficult to cultivate. The fields, meadows and orchards are all on slopes or terraces, and in some cases extend right up to the very rock faces of the higher mountains.

La cumbre is impressive in any season. Coniferous forests abound and a special silence seems to hang over the evergreen treetops. The rock formations with their different textures and colours are fascinating. Light and shadow dance along the sheer cliff faces and monoliths. The view from the peaks on a clear day is simply breathtaking. If you venture off the beaten track, into the tranquil heart of the uplands, you'll discover the hidden natural beauty of this island, the memory of which will stay with you for a long time to come. For those interested in natural history, Gran Canaria offers some unique species of flora, particularly in the mountain regions where the plant life is richer than you might at first suppose.

There are many tranquil spots in central Gran Canaria. The village of Tejeda is one of the loveliest

Some regions can only be reached in a jeep, though much of the area can be explored on foot. Don't worry about getting lost if you're tempted by an interesting-looking detour – the island is well served by a network of tracks throughout the interior. Some of these tracks twist and turn in the most fantastic manner through the mountains. They are known as *caminos reales*, or 'royal roads', which is a rather inappropriate name given that the majority of them are barely wide enough to allow two mules to pass. Until fairly recently, these tracks provided the only route of access to the outside world for many villages and isolated communities. In addition to these 'royal roads', there are a multitude of other tracks used by shepherds and goatherds. These are clearly laid out and easy to follow for the most part, but in places they have been covered over with

MARCO POLO SELECTION: THE INTERIOR

1 Pinar de Tamadaba
High alpine forests, vertiginous cliffs and, on clear days, spectacular views of Tenerife's highest peak (page 56)

2 Pinos de Gáldar
Rolling hills, green meadows and volcanic rock (page 57)

3 La Caldera de los Marteles
Gran Canaria's youngest volcanic crater lies just below the highest peak (page 58)

4 Carrizal de Tejeda
This charming ancient mountain hamlet clings to the steep slope like a swallow's nest (page 58)

5 Bienmesabe
A traditional almond dessert that is out of this world (page 58)

6 Llano de la Pez y Pargana
A five-star picnic spot near the Roque Nublo (page 59)

scree or rockfall and some have suffered badly from the effects of erosion.

ARTENARA

(**101/E4**) At 1,250 m above sea level, Artenara is the highest settlement on Gran Canaria. The population of this village is rapidly declining and today it is inhabited by only 1,119 hardy souls, making it not only the highest, but also the smallest village on Gran Canaria. The largest employer is ICONA, an organization dedicated to nature conservation and responsible for the reforestation, anti-erosion and fire-fighting measures implemented in the interior of the island.

SIGHTS

La Virgen de la Cuevita
Most of Artenara's inhabitants still live in caves, or rather caves with little house fronts built onto them. If you are approaching the village from the south on the rough asphalt road via Tejeda, from a distance these dwellings look like a row of birds' nests glued to the rock face. If you are curious to see the inside of these houses and get a feel for what it must be like to live in such surroundings, their occupants are usually quite willing to show visitors around. If you are lucky enough to be invited inside one of these converted cave dwellings, you'll be surprised to see that they're not primitive at all, despite what many a tour guide will have you believe. On the contrary, they all have electricity and running water and are equipped with all modern comforts. Kitchens are fully fitted, bathrooms are tiled and living rooms are complete with stereo system, video and TV. Marble floors lead to the bedrooms furnished with large beds. It all looks very comfortable indeed.

The view from these houses is incredible. To see it for yourself, pay a visit to *La Virgen de la Cuevita* (the virgin of the little cave) – patron saint of folk musicians and cyclists. The pretty little cave chapel is about 1 km from the village square, and can be reached only on foot. It was carved out of the volcanic rock (tufa), slabs of which serve as altar, chancel and confessional booths.

It's also worth paying a visit to the village church to see the 'constellations' carved out of wood on the ceiling. (If it's closed, ask for further information at the town hall across the road.)

RESTAURANT

Mesón la Silla

You get a great view of the unusual landscape from the terrace of this original cave restaurant. The setting is great, but the food is nothing to write home about. *Tel. 66 61 08; 10 am–6 pm daily; Category 2/3. Access only on foot, through a 100-m-long tunnel*

SHOPPING

All the shops, monuments and local businesses are crammed together in one small street, where all your needs are catered for. The post office, basilica, bar, mayor's office and taxi rank are all next door to one another and just a few yards further along you'll find a small supermarket (*tienda*) – the highest-situated supermarket! Halfway between the square and the chapel is the house of Ismael, a local stonemason who makes wonderful carvings from pieces of tree root.

The Cruz de Tejeda, which belongs to the state-run Parador chain

SURROUNDING AREA

Pinar de Tamadaba (101/D3–4)
It's only a few kilometres from the centre of Artenara to ★ *Pinar de Tamadaba*, the largest area of forest on the island. On warm days, the air here is filled with the scent of the scrubland bushes and resin from the pine trees. The road ends in a loop in the woods, which are punctuated with picnic areas, viewpoints and hiking trails, encouraging you to leave your car behind and explore the countryside on foot. There is a holiday camp (*campamento*) in the forest, which is occupied only during the summer months. The site stands next to a vertiginous mountain drop, which offers a magnificent view, but it's only worth making your way to this spot on a clear day, and even then there's no guarantee that you won't be suddenly engulfed in a thick cloud carried by the unpredictable trade winds. It is no sur-

Roque Nublo in the heart of Gran Canaria

prise that many of the pine branches have long beards of lichen. In any case, you can't be positive that you'll see the Pico de Teide, Tenerife's highest mountain, which often appears as just a smudge on the horizon. 'The Crown of Tenerife' is in fact the highest mountain of Spain – at 3,718 m, it is only 80 m lower than the highest mountain in Austria. On a clear day when you can see it standing alone in all its glory, towering above the sea, it's as impressive a sight as many in the Alps and, especially when silhouetted in dark violet against a pale pink evening sky, one that will stay in your memory for a long time.

Pinos de Gáldar **(101/E4)**
★ The landscape to the north-east of Artenara is a varied one of gently rolling hills and valleys with often verdant slopes. In the midst of it stands the *Pinos de Gáldar* – the name for a group of conifer woods – and on the road to Valleseco, to the left of it, towers a picture-book volcano. The slopes and fields are covered in a fine layer of volcanic ash.

This part of the island is a paradise for nature-lovers and keen walkers. The wild landscape and the variation in flora and fauna complement each other perfectly and it is difficult not to be moved by the sheer beauty of it all. Every so often you'll be startled by the sudden appearance of goats or sheep scampering over the rocks. A heavenly place!

If you're feeling adventurous, you should brave the road from Artenara via Lugajeros to Fagajesto. It narrows considerably beyond the last reservoir, at the rocky foot of the Tamadaba Plateau. In fact, it almost disappears, but, if you're careful, you can negotiate it quite safely. Then it snakes along the edge of a sheer cliff and, if you can bear to look, there are some great views of the Agaete Valley in the distance.

TEJEDA

(101/E5) This mountain village is the secret capital of the *Cumbre*. It's not a bad life for the approximately 2,500 people who live here. Their lovely village lies right at the heart of the island at a height of between 950 and 1,050 m. It is largely unspoilt and the setting and scenery inspires many a photographer. It is a popular destination for organized exursions, though you won't see many coaches parked. Tourists usually just pass through as their ultimate destination is not the village itself. They are making their way to *Cruz de Tejeda*, 5 km further up, on the high pass. This is where the real tourist business is carried out. Here, you'll find a grandiose complex in typical Canary Island style with towers, portals, gates, a courtyard, atrium and restaurant. You'll come across donkey-drivers with their animals, market stalls and souvenir stands. The whole complex was the brainchild of the multi-talented artist Néstor Martín Fernández de la Torre, who was also responsible for the *Pueblo Canario* in Las Palmas.

The country around Tejeda is replete with almond trees. The relatively high humidity means that a number of other fruits and vegetables can be successfully cultivated here. The soil is kept

In the spirit of Marco Polo

Marco Polo was the first true world traveller. He travelled with peaceful intentions forging links between the East and the West. His aim was to discover the world, and explore different cultures and environments without changing or disrupting them. He is an excellent role model for the travellers of today and the future. Wherever we travel we should show respect for other peoples and the natural world.

WWF

in place by a system of drystone dykes, a familiar sight on the landscape of this windy island.

SHOPPING

Many of the farmers' wives in Tejeda have made the treatment and preparation of almonds into something of an art. One of the local delicacies, which should definitely be sampled, is ★ *bienmesabe* (literally translated, it means 'how good it tastes'). It is a deliciously smooth cream made from grated almonds, lemon peel, egg yolk, sugar and water. It is used mainly as an accompaniment to desserts, as a topping for cakes or you can simply spread it on bread like jam.

RESTAURANT

Cruz de Tejeda
This is the only hotel on the island belonging to the state-run Parador chain. Its restaurant offers reasonable Hispano-Canarian cuisine. *12 noon–4:30 pm daily; Tel. 66 60 50; Category (R) 1/2*

HOTEL

El Refugio
This mountain hotel, next to the Cruz de Tejeda, offers breakfast and dinner. *10 rooms; Tel. 66 65 13; Fax 66 65 20; Category (H) 2/3*

SURROUNDING AREA

Ayacata (102/A6)
The mountain hamlet of Ayacata is a good resting place. It stands at the road junction halfway between San Bartolomé de Tirajana and Tejeda. There is a road that swings down from here towards Morgán that is popular with jeep drivers eager to test the performance of their vehicles on the rough, steep tracks. The reservoir lake, *La Presa de la Cueva de las Niñas*, is a popular spot amongst the locals. It is said to have been named after a grotto once famed as a spot for 'sinful' love-making. So the world's oldest profession was apparently not unfamiliar to the Canarians' ancestors.

La Caldera de los Marteles (102/C6)
★ It's well worth making a detour to *Caldera de los Marteles.* According to geologists, the last volcanic eruption, with rains of ash, took place here some 1,000 years ago.

Carrizal de Tejeda (101/D5)
★ To reach this tiny mountain village you will need to negotiate a fairly hair-raising road full of twists and turns. It is a quaint and unspoilt place where time seems to have stood still – a prime ex-

ample of a true Canarian rural community.

Pozo de las Nieves (102/B6)
To get to ⁂ *Pozo de las Nieves* (which means 'well of snow', so-called because in winter the peak is often covered in snow), you take the road to Roque Nublo and then turn right at the next crossroads (sharp left takes you to Cruz de Tejeda, semi-left to San Mateo and Las Palmas).

This road will lead you through a coniferous forest that has plenty of resting areas and picnic spots. The nicest one is the place situated in the ★ *Llano de la Pez y Pargana* area. From the summit of the Pozo de las Nieves (1,949 m) you get a fantastic view of the whole Tirajana Valley.

Roque Bentaiga (101/E5)
The majestic ⁂ *Roque Bentaiga* (1,412 m) stands about 5 km west of Tejeda. The basalt monolith was used by early inhabitants as a place for sacrificial ceremonies. Today, along with the *Cueva del Rey* (king's cave) just beyond, it's a popular destination for hikers and day trippers.

Roque Nublo (102/A6)
⁂ Halfway between San Bartolomé de Tirajana and Tejeda, another road bends round to the right at the small church with the tiny bell-tower. It then rises steeply and eventually leads you up to *Roque Nublo* (cloud rock), one of the island's most prominent landmarks, lauded in many a song. The monolith came into being as an 'extra', so to speak, some time during the second period of great volcanic activity on Gran Canaria. The base can be reached from the road on foot. Down below on the right, you can see the *Presa de los Hornos* reservoir glistening in the sun. Many visitors are under the impression that Roque Nublo is the highest peak on the island because it dominates the surrounding landscape so much. In fact, at 1,803 m, Roque Nublo is several dozen metres shorter than the neighbouring Pozo de las Nieves. Incidentally, *Coto de Caza*, as many signs in the area read, means hunting ground.

Old windmill in central Gran Canaria

Sandy beaches and sheltered bays

The hinterland of the island's south is reminiscent of the 'Wild West'

Particularly the older islanders divide Gran Canaria into four regions. As far as they are concerned, the by far largest is *El Sur* – the south. Yet when they refer to *El Sur*, they mean more than just a geographical area. The south actually includes the east and the west, in other words everything that's not the capital, the north and the central mountain massif. Thus, the south begins at Telde in the east, includes the airport and the steppe-like hilly landscape along the shore up to Arguineguín, encompassing all the tourist resorts between Bahía Feliz and Mogán and the wild rocky coast up to San Nicolás de Tolentino and beyond.

Anyone traversing *El Sur* immediately notices that this is an area with low precipitation (less than 100 litres per square metre per annum). Vegetation is accordingly sparse, much more arid than in the lush north. The plant life is comprised mainly of succulents, cacti and Canary date palms.

The imposing peaks of the sand dunes at Maspalomas

The main attractions of the coastal region are the long sandy beaches, the charming sheltered bays, the busy marinas and fishing harbours and the vast tourist resorts, with the wide selection of activities that have sprung up around them.

Even though the hinterland is less popular amongst tourists, there is a great deal here that deserves to be explored. The landscape is reminiscent of the 'Wild West' in many respects. The weather-beaten rock formations wouldn't look out of place in Colorado. You even encounter 'real' highwaymen offering refreshments and snacks by the roadside, including fruits and vegetables from the area. The climate in some areas is almost tropical, which favours the cultivation of tomatoes, bananas, lemons, mangoes, apricots, papayas and almonds.

The roads are generally in good condition, but if you want to venture off the beaten track you will need to have a jeep, or else travel on foot.

Beautiful winding and climbing roads, partly lined with eucalyptus trees, lead through villages and hamlets that have remained largely untouched by time.

Near the village of San Nicolás in the west, the island shows its stark side. Sheer cliffs, formed over millions of years into extraordinary shapes, drop abruptly down hundreds of metres to the sea. The inaccessibility of many areas here is the reason why, until a generation ago, *El Sur* was the most sparsely populated region in Gran Canaria. But as tourism worked to bring people to the area, new opportunities grew to help the locals make a better living. Consequently the population of many towns has increased considerably over the years. Although this trend is showing signs of slowing down, the area is still in a state of flux.

ARGUINEGUÍN

(**105/D5-6**) In the language spoken by the original inhabitants of Gran Canaria, Arguineguín means 'calm waters, mild breeze', which is a very fitting description of this lively fishing port. It lies in a sheltered bay with the gentle foothills of the mountains visible in the background. You can see Arguineguín's secret landmark from far away. The large silos of the 'most beautifully situated cement factory in the world' are directly on the shore of the Atlantic Ocean, some 12 km west of Maspalomas. Directly next to it, the Barranco de Arguineguín runs into a huge sea of banana trees. This is where the *Autopista del Sur*, the island's southern motorway, ends or begins, respectively. There are plans to extend it up to Morgán.

The town has undergone considerable expansion in the last few years – in all three dimensions. New buildings have gone up at such a rate that apparently there hasn't been enough time to clear away debris or to finish painting the façades.

Still, Arguineguín is a popular destination, not least because the appeal of this community of 3,500 lies more in its vitality and atmosphere than in its natural beauty. Islanders and foreign residents live side by side and are not segregated into separate communities as they are in Playa del Inglés, for example. The main areas where long-term residents and foreign businesspeople live side by side with tourists and retired people from Europe, particularly Scandinavia and Germany, are *Patalavaca* and *Los Caideros* (to the west of the town, on a steep shoreline) as well as *Canarios I* (beyond the busy main road).

Most interesting is the ✪ Harbour District. Between the simple houses on the tongue of land that extends into a large jetty, you can smell freshly laundered clothes and the various catches of the day.

RESTAURANTS

Arguineguín is one of the best places on the island to eat fish. It deserves star rating for the sheer number of seafood restaurants and snack bars (some better than others) it has to offer. Comfortable, rustic atmosphere with menus offering a wide selection of meals.

Los Canarios I

Fish and meat are of excellent quality. The stuffed sole is partic-

MARCO POLO SELECTION: THE SOUTH

1 **Soria**
A young hippie community by the island's largest reservoir (page 64)

2 **Güigüi**
One of the most beautiful sandy and secluded beaches, which can be reached only by boat or on foot (page 76)

3 **Tennis Hotel**
A magnificent hotel with tennis courts above the Palmitos Park (page 67)

4 **Hao**
Tucked away behind the museum with the most Canarian character is this traditional Canarian restaurant. All kinds of home-made dishes can be savoured in a wonderful atmosphere (page 86)

5 **La Bodeguilla Juananá**
This unique cheese shop in Puerto de Mogán also offers authentic Canarian arts and crafts items (page 73)

ularly good. *C/Princesa Guyarmina; Tel. 15 06 67; 6 pm–12 midnight Wed–Sat and Mon, 1 pm–12 midnight Sun; Category 2/3*

Marino Chico
Freshly caught fish and a friendly service, in the Ancora shopping centre. *6–11 pm Thurs–Tues, also 12 noon–4 pm Tues and Sun; Tel. 73 56 69; Category 2/3*

SHOPPING

Many specialist shops and relatively good-value supermarkets, too. The weekly market is held on Tuesdays and there is a fish market every morning at the harbour.

HOTELS

Aquamarina
Beautiful garden and small private beach, four tennis courts, elegant apartments and bungalows (altogether 170 beds). *Barranco de la Verga; Tel. 73 52 00 and 73 51 25; Fax 73 61 25; Category (A) 1 (B) 1*

La Canaria
A very luxurious establishment (five stars) of the Steigenberger group, large garden and landscaped pool area next to the water (private bay). 216 double rooms (from 40 sq m), all with a sea view and a balcony; very comfortably and tastefully furnished.

Two tennis courts (artificial surface and flood-lit), a squash court, motor boats, water-skiing, jet-skiing and child care are available during your stay.

One of the ten best hotels on the Canary Islands. Three minutes' drive from the centre of Arguineguín. *Barranco de la Verga s/n; Tel. 15 04 00; Fax 15 10 03; Category (H) 1*

Pensión León
Basic accommodation, shared kitchen facilities, only 100 m from the beach. Twelve double rooms, three singles. *C/ Miguel Marrero 27; Tel. 15 02 35; Category (G) 2.* If closed, try the Hostál Estévez around the corner.

SPORTS & LEISURE

Many of the locals still make a living from deep-sea fishing, but also organize fishing trips for tourists. All foreign visitors are required to obtain a special fishing permit from the Marine Authorities in Las Palmas. Yet, knowing the *patrón*, the captain of the boat you want to go out in, is often enough as well.

Hobby anglers will find everything they need for their fishing trip at *Casa Pedro, C/ Miguel Marrero.*

BEACHES

Playa de Arguineguín
Central beach with a mixture of fine sand, pebbles and some rocks. It is small (about 200 m long and 20 m wide) and unfortunately it's often dirty. There is a somewhat dilapidated seawater pool to the west at *Playa de la Lajilla* with a small beach suitable for sunbathing. The water here is relatively clean.

Playa de Patalavaca
This small fine-sand beach lies along a built-up part of the coast, about 2 km west of Arguineguín. The water here is sometimes slightly polluted.

SURROUNDING AREA

Soria (105/D2)
★ The biggest dam on the island is in the upper reaches of the Arguineguín Valley. It was completed in 1971, but the reservoir, *Presa de Soria,* was never filled. A group of young people formed a community in the abandoned houses that had been vacated to make way for the reservoir. The population of the 'Free Republic of Soria' fluctuates depending on the current mood in the 'scene', but there can be anywhere from 1 to 100 residents there. In the winter months, there are many who simply want a break from their roommates or significant others for a few weeks. Good old-fashioned island cuisine is offered at *Casa Fernando: 10 am–6 pm daily except Mon; Tel. 73 58 34; Category 3.* (Their goulash *carne en salsa* is especially good.) Tip: The owners will be more than willing to tell you about some of the best walking and hiking tracks in the area. Experienced walkers should consider climbing the nearby *Montaña de Tauro.*

Barranco de Arguineguín (105/D2–5)
The *Barranco de Arguineguín* is a deep valley that stretches northwards from the coast for some 20 km, with cultivated gardens, fields, wilderness areas and a few scattered settlements, one of which is *Cercado de Espino*, where a butcher offers home-made food in his castle *Ramón.* The road gradually gets steeper and twists and winds its way up to the tiny mountain hamlet of *Barranquillo Andrés.*

ARINAGA

(107/E3) Most people catch their first sight of this rapidly expanding village from the plane as it makes its final approach before landing on Gran Canaria. Arinaga lies on the coast about 8 km south of the airport. The flight path runs just north of the village.

SIGHTS

Wind propellers
On the outskirts of the village there is a pilot scheme to test the viability of solar and wind energy for the desalination of sea water, with about 50 wind propellers.

RESTAURANT

La Farola
Restaurant with its own private lobster farm. *C/Alcalá Gallano (at the start of the great harbour breakwater), Puerto de Arinaga; 1 pm–12 midnight Mon–Sat, 1–6 pm Sun; Tel. 18 02 24; Category 1/2*

BEACHES

The water in many parts of the bay is crystal clear. The brown sandy beach is 400 m long and rocky in places. A breakwater protects the bay from any swell and there is a pleasant sea-front promenade. The coastline around Arinaga is popular amongst divers.

SURROUNDING AREA

Agüimes **(107/D–E2)**
The old church is visible from a distance. With its large, round dome, it looks like a mosque, an impression that is reinforced by the landscape's north African feel.

Cuatro Puertas **(103/E6)**
The 200-m-high *Montaña de las cuatro puertas* (mountain of the four gates) is on the road from Ingenio to Telde. There is a cave on the northern side with four rectangular entrances. The grotto used to serve as a place where people could assemble.

Guayadeque **(107/C1-D2)**
With its combination of volcanic landscape and abundant flora, the *Barranco de Guayadeque* is one of the loveliest gorges on the island. The steep slopes have more holes in them than Swiss cheese. Some of the caves serve as dwellings that are still inhabited today. A visit to the cave chapel is an absolute must. The loveliest 'cave restaurant' is called *Tagoror* (cul-de-sac) at the end of the gorge. The road to Guayadeque is signposted from the upper part of Ingenio. A popular picnic spot amongst the locals.

Ingenio **(107/D–E2)**
Ingenio, about 8 km west of the airport, is the arts and crafts centre of Gran Canaria, or so the mayor of the town with a population of about 25,000 maintains. The many new houses, however, are not exactly indicative of a great sense of aesthetics. The *Museo de Piedras y Artesanía* gives you an overview of what Igenio has to offer in Canarian arts and crafts. The adjoining embroidery school is also of interest. *C/ Çamino Real de Gando; 8 am–6.30 pm daily; Tel. 78 11 24; Admission free*

MASPALOMAS OASIS

(106/A-B5-6) The Oasis of Maspalomas, as it has always been called, lies on the southernmost tip of the island and can be reached via three avenidas. The well-worn cliché of 'sun, sea and sand' could have been coined for this haven. The former paradise for bird life (more than 30 bird species, amongst them even vultures and ospreys, used to live here and migrate to this area during the winter months) is located in the centre of an old palm grove at the edge of a lagoon, which is unfortunately not as clean as it once was. *Las Dunas de Maspalomas*, a protected area that has been designated as a breathtakingly beautiful nature reserve, borders the northern bank of the lagoon. The most prominent landmark of this special area is the 56-m-high lighthouse. *El Faro de Maspalomas* marks the most south-easterly point of the Canarian archipelago.

RESTAURANT

L'Orangerie (Hotel Palm Beach)
This hotel offers French food at its most delicious. Michelin star. *Avda Oasis s/n; Tel. 14 08 06; 7.30–11 pm Mon–Wed, Fri and Sat; Category 1*

HOTELS

Casa Epikurea
Small, quiet bungalow estate, with a friendly atmosphere. *Campo Internacional, Avda Touroperador Cosmos; Tel. 14 15 78; Category (B) 3*

Hotel Faro
The only hotel in Maspalomas with direct access to the sea. 188 en suite double rooms. The atmosphere is less snooty than in the comparable Palm Beach Hotel. *Plaza del Faro; Tel. 14 23 42; Fax 14 19 40; Category (H) 1*

Palm Beach
This hotel is superbly located in a palm-tree oasis, less than 200 m from the dunes. The exclusive décor and excellent service, which are based on the classical style of the grand hotels of Europe, give this 700-bed establishment a character all its own. We recommend that you insist on a room above the ground floor overlooking the pool and garden. *Tel. 14 08 06; Fax 14 18 08; Category (H) 1*

SPORTS & LEISURE

Maspalomas, like the rest of the Costa Canaria, has a lot to offer in the way of different sport and leisure activities, with plenty of good facilities for tennis, golf, diving, surfing and more.

Golf
The golf course at Maspalomas is located at Campo Internacional. In recent years, it has undergone a complete face lift and all 18 holes can be played (6,220 m, par 73). The club offers non-golfers the chance to get a feel for the game and you don't need to have proof of membership of a club back home to play here, as many other golf clubs in Europe do. The prices are reasonable as well, being well below the European average.

It will cost you 2,500 ptas for a half-hour lesson with a professional, 9,000 ptas for a round of golf, 1,700 ptas to hire clubs and 500 ptas for a trolley. There are no caddies. *Tel. 76 25 81; Avda Neckermann; 8 am–8 pm (summer), 8 am–6 pm (winter); Reservations recommended*

Squash
About 200 m from the golf course are three well-equipped squash courts. *Tel. 76 74 47; 145 ptas per hour*

Tennis
A number of hotel and apartment complexes have their own private tennis facilities, and some of them will hire out their courts (*pistas de tenis*) to non-residents. The *Ibero Oasis* in Maspalomas is one of them. It has four clay courts, all floodlit, which can be booked at the porter's desk. *Tel. 14 14 48; 1,100 ptas per hour; lessons available at a rate of 4,900 ptas for 45 minutes*

BEACHES

Playa de Maspalomas
This broad beach is one mass of undulating dunes. The imposing mountains of golden sand in the Maspalomas Oasis can reach a height of over 30 m. The sea swell and wind can be fairly strong here. The water is very clean, but the constant swell stirs up the sea bed and makes the sea appear slightly dirty.

SURROUNDING AREA

Monte León **(106/A4)**
Maspalomas has never had a shortage of illustrious guests. Its three luxury hotels – Oasis, Faro and Palm Beach – are the most exclusive on the island and have long been popular amongst the political, showbiz and sporting elite. Yet, the district with villas where many VIPs stay is in a slightly more secluded area, on the slopes of 500-m-high Monte León (between the Maspalomas gorge and the Barranco de Palmitos, which begins below El Tablero). To reach this wealthy district, you pass through the village of *Montaña la Data* on the road to Monte León.

It's a favourite spot amongst locals who come here to dine in the rustic *El Labrador* restaurant garden *(Tel. 14 12 88; 1–4 pm and 6.30–11.30 pm daily except Mon; Category 2/3).*

Palmitos Park **(106/A4)**
First established in the early 1970s in the Barranco de los Palmitos, a barren rocky landscape 12 km above Maspalomas, this park has become one of the best wildlife reserves in the world, complete with orchid gardens and palm trees. It is home to over 300 different species of tropical bird, which compete with a spectacular collection of exotic plants for the enthusiastic visitors' attention. *Tel. 14 03 66; 9 am–6 pm daily; Bus no. 70, every ten minutes from Playa del Inglés; Admission: 1,975 ptas (adults), 1,150 ptas (children) including parrot show, butterfly house and marine aquarium*

Playa de las Meloneras **(106/A6)**
There is only one track down to this sand-and-pebble beach, which is about 500 m long: a turn-off on the main road from Maspalomas to Arguineguín. There is a restaurant by the water's edge that also hires out deckchairs and parasols. Unfortunately, the sea here is often plagued by algae that float on the surface. During the summer season, the beach is popular amongst campers. The hills behind the beach are currently under development and it's accordingly noisy, but you can find quieter, smaller sandy bays in the area between Meloneras and Arguineguín. Most of them can be reached only on foot.

Tennis Hotel **(106/A4)**
Some 600 m above Palmitos Park you will find another oasis – this

one is for keen tennis players and anyone who wants to relax and enjoy the solitude of the mountains. The ★ *Helga Masthoff* hotel has 60 beds, six AstroTurf courts, a sauna, a swimming pool, a restaurant and a bar. *Barranco de los Palmitos; Tel. 14 21 00; Fax 14 11 14; Category (H) 2*

MOGÁN

(104/C2-3) Mogán, a picturesque mountain village that nestles in the upper reaches of the Barranco de Mogán, is a prosperous place. The reconstructed plaza, the new town hall, the little park with its open-air stage – everywhere, one senses the village's aspiration to look its best. In the basalt village square, pieces of marble shimmer. On the outskirts are farmhouses and villas.

The not quite 700 inhabitants of Mogán enjoy a fairly high standard of living. All members of the family tend to work – father, mother, sons and daughters – in their own shops, in construction or by harvesting the produce cultivated on their own land where, thanks to the favourable climate, crops can be grown all year round.

The 12-km-long valley benefits from the subtropical climate that allows systematic cultivation of papayas, oranges, avocados and aubergines. The entire southwest corner of the island, from Arguineguín, through Puerto Rico to Puerto de Mogán and beyond, comes under the administrative authority of Mogán. The beautiful *Costa Mogán* has become increasingly popular amongst tourists, and can accommodate up to 30,000 visitors.

RESTAURANTS

Acaymo
Pleasantly rural atmosphere, fresh fish, charcoal grill, substantial Hispano-Canarian cuisine. The *tapas variadas* (a selection of appetizers) are particularly good. *Directly on the main street; Tel. 56 92 63; 12 noon–10.30 pm daily except Mon; Category 3*

Pub Düsseldorf
This is where the assemblymen and gendarmes sip their breakfast coffee. The kitchen confines itself to preparing snacks and *tapas*. Dancing for young people often on weekends from 10 pm. *C/General Franco (diagonally opposite the mayor's office, next to the savings bank); Tel. 56 92 73; 8 am–4.30 pm Mon–Thurs, 10 pm–4.30 am Sat and Sun*

HOTELS

Mogán has a surprisingly large number of private rooms and holiday apartments for rent, on a daily, weekly or even seasonal basis. Ask at any of the bars for information about what's on offer. It's easy to talk to the locals, who are open and friendly.

Pension Doña Mina
Four double rooms with rustic atmosphere in a romantic setting, with cooking facilities. *Carretera General 6; Tel. 56 90 41; Category (G) 1*

ENTERTAINMENT

El Laurel
Popular amongst the locals who congregate here in the evenings. No food, but rooms are available. *C/San José (under the tall eucalyptus tree); 9 am–11 pm daily*

SURROUNDING AREA

Pajonales **(105/D-E1)**
About 2 km above Mogán, a small road branches off into the interior. Jeep drivers love this road, whose surface is pitted and uneven and runs along some pretty hair-raising precipitous drops. The scenery is fantastic – sheer rock faces, reservoirs and age-old shepherd's paths. It is a haven for hikers and a designated nature reserve under the name *Pajonales*. One of its major attractions is the endemic Mocán tree. A member of the laurel family, it has beautiful white blossoms in winter. Its cherry-like, dark red fruit is not only edible, but the juice can be fermented and made into a delicious aqua vitae. No wonder it's revered by the locals!

Tasarte **(104/B2-3)**
The *Barranco de Tasarte* between Mogán and San Nicolás is a beautiful, green and cultivated valley that's well worth a detour. At the mouth of the *barranco*, there is a long, stony beach. It's not really suitable for bathing, but does have a respectable fish restaurant, *Oliva*, which serves basic, but good, food. *11 am–5 pm Tues–Sun; Tel. 89 43 58; Category 3*

PLAYA DEL INGLÉS

(**106/B5-6**) This resort is the most popular destination on Gran Canaria after Las Palmas. It starts just beyond the town of San Augustín, but, on a plateau some 30 m high, it broadens out like a wedge the further south you go.

RESTAURANTS

Pepe el Breca
This is arguably *the* seafood restaurant in the south of the island. Set in an old county house, it is very well run, and has a comfortable, pleasant atmosphere. Try the *viejas a la espalda* (parrotfish) or the *cherne* (bream) coated in sea salt. *In the San Fernando District, Carretera Fataga s/n; Tel. 77 26 37; 1–4 pm and 7 pm–12 midnight Mon–Sat; Advance booking recommended; Category 1/2*

Wences
This popular bar offers *tapas* and a set menu that changes daily. *Avda de Gáldar; Tel. 76 87 89; 9 am–11 pm Mon–Sat, kitchen 1 pm–4 pm; Category 3*

Forest fires

When you are exploring the island, take care not to throw cigarette ends out of the car or leave bottles or glass lying around – they can easily cause the forest or scrubland to catch fire, either directly or through the sun's rays on the glass. Camp-fires should also be avoided as should the use of lanterns on night-time picnics. The island's mountain areas are very dry, especially in summer. Heath fires near newly cultivated areas can destroy the hard work of a decade in a matter of hours. Another request: If you want to take a souvenir of the island's flora with you, then shake a few seeds out of old blooms or pods rather than taking living plants.

HOTELS

Buenaventura Playa

Aimed at young people and those young at heart who are ready to meet other people. Plenty of activities on offer – sports, games, and sheer fun and adventure. Shuttle bus to the beach or a 30-minute walk. 724 double rooms. *Plaza Ansite; Tel. 76 16 50; Fax 76 83 48; Category (H) 2/3*

Casa de Huéspedes Residencia San Fernando

Centrally located in the district of San Fernando. Sixty basic double rooms, shared bathrooms. Not to everyone's taste. *C/La Palma 16; Tel. 76 39 06; Category (G) 2*

Rented accommodation arrangement

The following organizations arrange rented accommodation in apartments, bungalows and holiday homes:

Canaridata, Canarian Reservation Center; C/León y Castillo, 89; Tel. 24 65 19; Fax 29 21 42

Haffner Rentals, C/Roma 16; Tel. 77 26 92; Fax 77 03 89

Wolfgang Aretz Rentals, Bungalow Granada no. 7E; Tel. 76 29 37 or 76 50 22; Fax 76 64 64

Sandy Beach

The hotel is only about 200 m from the beach. The architecture is Moorish in style and the hotel provides four–five-star comfort with three-star service. 256 double rooms with en suite marble bathroom, balcony, telephone, music, safe deposit box. Floodlit tennis court. Entertaining animation programmes as well as a children's pool and play area and buffet restaurant. *Avda Alfereces Provisionales; Tel. 77 27 26; Fax 76 72 52; Category (H) 1/2*

SPORTS & LEISURE

Cycling & motorcycling

You can hire mountain bikes, mopeds and motorbikes from the *Sun Fun Motorcenter, Gran Chaparral Shopping Centre; Tel. 76 38 29. Motos Tivoli* also have a good selection of motorbikes for hire. *Edificio Prisma, Avda España 7; Tel. and Fax 76 34 17.* Keen bikers should check out *Easy Rider Rentals,* which offers a range of Harley Davidsons for hire (*Tel. and Fax 76 98 46*).

Miniature golf

One of the nicest courses is in the *San Valentin Park* bungalow com-

Playa del Inglés – a tourist Mecca

plex *(near the Hotel Neptuno): 9 am–11 pm daily; Admission: 200 ptas (adults), 125 ptas (children)*

BEACHES

Playa del Inglés

This broad stretch of light-brown to ochre sand, which slopes gently down into the water, is Gran Canaria's number one tourist beach. Several kilometres long, it starts off fairly narrow and gradually widens the further south one goes.

ENTERTAINMENT

Casa Antonio

The most traditional dance and entertainment venue in the south is located in a disused barn on land belonging to the aristocratic Del Castillo family. A wide variety of folk music and traditional dance music is played here. The programme caters mainly for tourists. You can also eat here, but although they don't skimp on the portions, the quality of the food is nothing to write home about. The heart of the place is the entertainer Don Antonio. *San Fernando–Playa del Inglés; Tel. 76 72 25; 12 noon– 12 midnight daily*

Cita

Playa del Inglés has plenty to offer in the way of entertainment and activity (including ten-pin bowling), but by far the best place to seek out the action is the Cita shopping centre and beer village. *Between Avda Francia and Avda Alemania*

Discos

The selection of nightclubs and dance venues in and around Playa del Inglés is overwhelming. The best thing to do is to try a number of them out on the first or second evening on your holiday until you find the one that suits you the best. Here is a list of some of the pubs and discos in Playa del Inglés you could put to the test: *Garage Pub, Pascha Sascha's, Pacha Pub, Joy, Hard Rock Café, Chic, Life, Boney M., Belle Epoque* (more of a dance hall for those no longer as young as the disco crowd), *Rainbow, California* and *Hawaian Tasca.*

If you don't find what you're looking for amongst this lot, then chances are you'll have to go to Las Palmas to find a venue that's more to your taste. Remember, don't turn up too early as most of the discos don't really get going until after midnight. The gay scene is centred around the *Yumbo* shopping centre.

Oscar's Pub

Oscar's Pub, to the right of the IFA hotel *Dunamar* facing the promenade, has become one of the trendiest and most popular places in Playa del Inglés. The décor is a tasteful blend of wood, glass and brass. The owner has succeeded in creating an elegant, glamorous and sophisticated atmosphere. *Avda Helsinki 8; Tel. 77 07 62; from 7 pm daily*

INFORMATION & SHOPPING

Centro Insular de Turismo

The island's main tourist information centre. *Avda España (next to the main entrance of Yumbo shopping centre); Tel. 76 25 91; Fax 76 78 48; English spoken; 9 am–9 pm Mon–Fri, 9 am–2 pm Sat, closed on Sundays and holidays.* In the same

Hotel Palm Beach in Maspalomas Oasis – it makes good the promise its name implies

building, there is a state-run artisan centre, the *tienda de artesanía*, with genuine Canary Island arts-and-crafts items on sale (*10 am–1 pm and 4–7 pm Mon–Fri*).

SURROUNDING AREA

Fataga/ Mundo Aborigen (106/B2–4)

If you want to get an insight into what life was once like in a typical island village, then it's worth making the two-hour round trip to Fataga. As an added bonus, you get to see quite a bit of the island along the way. The journey starts from the 'Local Quarter' of San Fernando. About 6 km down the road, you'll spot Fred Flintstone waiting to welcome you to El Mundo Aborigen, a detailed reconstruction of an ancient Canary Island settlement. Even if you're not all that interested in Stone-Age life, it's worth visiting just for the fantastic view you get of the Costa Canaria. From here, the hotels and resort complexes in the distance look like children's building bricks strewn along the coastline. *El Mundo Aborigen, Carretera Playa del Inglés–Fataga, 6 km; 9 am–6 pm daily; Admission: 1,200 ptas (adults), 600 ptas (children)*

Tablero/Ayagaures (106/A3–5)

El Tablero, formerly a hamlet where workers on the nearby *finca* (country estate) used to be housed, is now a rapidly expanding village. However, life here is still relatively rural and tranquil, at least when compared with life in San Fernando. The Maspalomas Dunes are only about five minutes away by car. The journey takes you through the lower reaches of the Maspalomas Valley. From here, you can take the side road into the *Barranco de Ayagaures* at the end of which you'll come across a number of scattered settlements and two reservoirs.

PUERTO DE MOGÁN

(**104/B4**) This new marina and fishing harbour in the south-western corner of the island has received much critical acclaim. Such innovation had never been seen before on the island, and even the most critical opponent of the concrete-box tourist development on Gran Canaria is enthusiastic about this place, which has earned itself the name 'Little Venice'. A lot of thought and research went into the architectural design and its relationship to the environment, and the result is a development that is both individual in character and perfectly in tune with its surroundings. The well-proportioned, two-storey terraced houses, the attractive courtyards with basalt paving and flower beds, the pedestrianized alleyways and paths with bridges and old-fashioned street lamps, the typical Canary Island wooden balconies, the colourful walls of the houses, the carefully tended front gardens with their volcanic soil and abundant bougainvillea, the hidden corners and inner courtyards – all these elements blend together to create a unique atmosphere. The chic marina was built in the area where fishing boats used to be moored until recently. A semi-circular harbour wall was landscaped and dredged to provide an attractive but functional marina. The second (and final) phase was completed in 1989.

RESTAURANTS

La Bodeguilla Juananá

★ This pleasant, comfortable and tastefully decorated restaurant offers all Canarian brands of cheese (to go if you want), wines from the entire archipelago, hearty hams and country sausages, authentic local arts-and-crafts items and both traditional and Canary Island nouvelle cuisine. Yes, that too exists nowadays. The owner will be only too happy to explain exactly what this *nueva cocina canaria* is all about. *Tel. 56 50 44; 7 pm–12 midnight daily except Mon, open during the day at irregular hours, 12 noon–3 pm Fri; Category 2*

Sunsets and starry nights

Star-gazing is dependent on weather conditions and circumstances that unfortunately are seldom as good as we'd like them to be. Either it's cloudy or hazy, the moon's too bright or we just don't have the time. However, here on the Canary Islands, the conditions are nearly always favourable. The stars shine brightly in the crystal-clear skies, particularly the North Star, which is considerably nearer to the horizon here as the island lies closer to the Tropic of Cancer. Mercury and Venus are also more clearly visible from here and can be observed just before sunrise or right after sunset, while the most beautiful sunsets can be seen between Puerto de Mogán and Agaete.

La Caracola
'The Seashell' is undoubtedly one of the best places to eat on Gran Canaria. At the same time it is one of the smallest and most expensive restaurants in all of Spain. Specialities of the house include fresh tuna and swordfish, shark and shellfish. *In the marina; Tel. 56 54 86; from 7 pm daily (closed in the summer); Advance booking recommended; Category 1*

Tu Casa
An old country house right on the beach, with a large terrace overlooking the water. The fruits and vegetables come from the proprietors' own *finca.* Ask for freshly caught fish (*pescado fresco*). The papaya dessert is also highly recommended. *Playa de Mogán; 12 noon–9 pm Mon–Wed; Tel. 56 50 78; Category 2/3*

Mamma Mia
Swiss-Italian cuisine, good pizzas and pasta dishes. *Playa de Mogán (next to the savings bank); Tel. 56 54 24; 12 noon–10 pm Tues–Sat, Sun only lunchtime; Category 2/3*

SHOPPING

Fish market
You can cast a glance at the *Pescadería Mogán*, the busy fish mar-

An aubergine field near Mogán

ket near the village square, and soak up the atmosphere. If you have cooking facilities, you can pick up some fresh fish (*pescada fresca*) at bargain prices.

Gallery

The Danish artist Lykke Vigen runs two galleries in Playa de Mogán, one of which is right in the main square, where you can buy attractive watercolours depicting Mogán and related themes. Reproductions start at around 500 ptas. *Art Plaza, Riviera del Carmen 10; 11 am–8 pm daily*

Market

A market is held every Friday in the square and surrounding streets.

HOTELS

You can ask for information about available accommodation in any bar. In Playa de Mogán itself, some of the locals rent out their own private rooms, apartments and studios.

The harbour district has altogether 240 apartments, holiday homes and a charming hotels with 120 beds.

Bartolo

The owner of this establishment is a legend in the village. He's also a specialist for creating feasts replete with paella and tequila. Ten small rooms. *Located a little outside (seven minutes on foot) in the district of Lomo Quiebre; Tel. 56 54 59; Category (G) 2 (R) 3*

Casa Lila

Nine rustic-style holiday apartments. Just outside town and two minutes from the beach. Recommended for individualists. *Tel. and Fax 56 57 29; Category (A) 2/3*

Hotel Club de Mar

Right on the seafront. Comfortable, pleasant rooms with balcony and sea views. Swimming pool, restaurant. *Tel. 56 50 66 or 56 50 65; Fax 56 54 34; Category (H) 2*

Salvador

Guest house in the heart of the fishing village with 12 double rooms and two studios. *Information and registration in the Salvador tapas bar (diagonally opposite the small church); Tel. 56 50 76 or 56 53 74; Category (G) 2 (A) 3*

Hotel Taurito Playa

New luxury hotel right on the Playa Taurito with 402 double rooms, each with a sea view; enormous salt-water swimming pool by the entrance (open to non-residents too for a fee!). Beautiful tropical garden on the cliffs. *Tel. 56 54 00; Fax 56 55 66; Category (H) 2*

BEACHES

Playa de Mogán

This man-made sandy beach, which is 300 m long and 30 m wide, slopes gently down to the sea and is safe for children. A natural stone wall protects the bay from excessive swell, but the drawback is that the water tends to be somewhat murky as the ebb and flow is restricted. The ruins of the old quay walls lie beyond the rocky outcrop known as *La Puntilla*, and further north there are some wonderful grottoes and rock formations – an ideal spot for experienced divers. The water here is completely clear.

Playa de Taurito

This natural beach is only about three minutes' drive from neighbouring Puerto de Mogán and about 350 m long and up to 70 m wide. Taurito was once a Mecca for aficionados of nude bathing. Today, the area is more built up and is very popular amongst locals on weekends and in summer.

SPORTS & LEISURE

Sailing and water sports

Information centre and equipment for hire (charter boats, day trips, sailing equipment and nautical goods): *Paradise Yachting in the fishing harbour, Unit 96; Tel. 56 55 90; Fax 56 55 28; English spoken.* The experience of a new thrill is offered: tandem parachuting from a height of 3,000 m.

Submarine

Exciting underwater excursions in a real yellow submarine. Great outing for kids. *Several daily departures from the big Mole; Tel. 56 51 08*

ENTERTAINMENT

La Taberna del Puerto

Draws a young, international crowd. Good music (plenty of jazz). Specialities of the house: fruit juices and fruit salads. *Open at irregular hours; on the promenade*

INFORMATION

Apartamentos Puerto de Mogán

Provides all kinds of information on accommodation and car rental. *Information Office, Future Comerce S. A., Unit X124; Tel. 56 56 72; Fax 56 56 18*

Port Authority

Provides information on sailing. 220 berths for sailing and motorboats up to 25 m in length, electricity, water and meteorological station. English spoken. *Puerto de Mogán S. A., Torre Control (at harbour entrance); Tel. 56 56 68; Fax 56 50 24 (English spoken)*

SURROUNDING AREA

Güigüi **(104/A1)**

The so-called 'Wild West' of the island offers fantastic views that will take your breath away. Many people consider ★ Güigüi to be *the* ultimate beach. With fine golden sand, it is several hundred metres long and several dozen wide, depending on the tide. The water is crystal clear and every shade of blue imaginable. The swell is exhilarating and raging crested waves thunder onto the shore. It's the classic island paradise. The steep cliffs surrounding the beach provide the perfect backdrop to such a dramatic set. But, strangely, this beach is almost always deserted. The fact that you can get there only on foot or by boat may have something to do with this. Getting there on foot from either Tasartico or San Nicolás de Tolentino can be strenuous and somewhat dangerous and is only really recommended for experienced walkers. A good head for heights is essential as are sturdy walking boots, hiking equipment, food supplies and fresh water. The route involves a fair bit of climbing and scrambling over rocks and scree, and the trip there and back can take anywhere from five to eleven hours, depending on the conditions. Therefore, this

Colourful fishing boats moor alongside impressive luxury yachts in Puerto de Mogán

is not a destination for a casual day trip or for inexperienced walkers who simply want to prove to themselves that they have guts. There is also an easier way to reach Güigüi: you can simply ask a skipper in Puerto de Mogán or Puerto Rico to take you there and pick you up again. But be prepared to pay about 1,700 ptas for a return trip. For more detailed information call *Paradise Yachting, Tel. 56 55 90.* Bear in mind that there's no landing stage at Güigüi, so you have to be able to swim ashore. Make sure that any equipment you take is well packed in waterproof containers.

Playa de Veneguera (104/B3)
There is a private track (closed to traffic) that leads from the district of Lomo Quiebre through the neighbouring valley to Playa de Veneguera. The walk takes between 4 and 5 hours there and back. A new holiday resort is being built at Playa de Veneguera for the next millennium.

Veneguera (104/B3)
It's worth making a short detour to visit the village of Veneguera, just to sample the delicious goat stew usually served in generous portions in both village bars. Ask for *carne de cabra en salsa.* Another remarkable feature here are the huge, cactus-like euphorbia plants that dominate the village landscape. Nowhere else on the island do they reach such a height or grow in such profusion. A word of caution: if you come into contact with a broken stem or spike, make sure the milky sap that oozes out doesn't come into contact with your eyes, or you'll suffer hours of excruciating pain.

PUERTO RICO

(104/C5) Puerto Rico is located at the *barranco* of the same name in the island's south-west, the area where you can most rely on the weather being lovely. At first sight, the place comes as a bit of a shock: the landscape is dominated by modern holiday blocks and tourist resorts, with concrete everywhere you look. From a distance, the piles of buildings look like a termite's nest. There are more than 25,000 tourist beds crammed into this narrow space and the sea of concrete is spreading out to neighbouring valleys – this is no longer in any relation to the size of the beach.

If you stop and take a closer look, however, you'll find that Puerto Rico does have some hidden charms. The inner valley itself is beautiful – an oasis of lush tropical flora and neat flower-filled gardens. It has its own public swimming pool, a range of restaurants, tennis courts, a children's play area, a miniature golf course and squash courts – in short, everything you need for a classic seaside holiday, and in the proper proportions. Even the buildings with just a few storeys fit into this attractive picture.

The two marinas are also very impressive. Puerto Rico was one of the first resorts on Gran Canaria to be fully developed for tourism and the marinas played a large part in its attracting new business. As a result, Puerto Rico has become the water sports capital of the island and the choice of aquatic activities on offer is endless. Another first for Puerto Rico, the 'rich port', is that it is so far the only area to have perfected the process of desalination. The water that flows from your taps will almost certainly be sea water that has been purified. Even the entire waste water supply is repurified and used to water the parks and gardens.

RESTAURANTS

Don Quijote

High-quality meat and fish dishes. The owner, Don Florencio, is a master chef. The *solomillo Puerto Rico* (sirloin steak flambé) is highly recommended, as is the country-style rabbit and exceptional paella. Very pleasant atmosphere. *Edificio Porto, Units 11 + 12, Novo; Tel. 56 09 01; 2 pm–12 midnight daily except Sun; Category 2/3*

The following restaurants also offer solid Spanish, Canarian and international food: *Henry's, Oliver's, Cristina* and *Casa Zamora; Category 2/3.*

SHOPPING

There is a ✪ market every Friday in Puerto de Mogán. A lovely way to come here is by boat – an excursion in itself. Líneas Salmón is the name of the ferry that runs from Puerto Rico to Puerto de Mogán. The return trip costs 1,000 ptas. The departure point is the harbour wall opposite the beach. The ferry sails daily, at the following times: Puerto Rico: 11 am – noon – 1 pm – 2 pm – 3 pm – 4 pm.

Puerto de Mogán: 11.45 am – 12.45 pm – 1.45 pm – 2.45 pm – 3.45 pm – 4.45 pm. The boat sails close to the coast and the journey takes about half an hour each way. Not even the locals tire of seeing their island from the water and you'll most certainly find it a memorable trip. You can purchase your ticket on the boat.

Another possibility is to go from Puerto Rico to Arguineguín and back. A roundtrip costs 700 ptas. Departure times from Puerto Rico are: 10.30 am – 12.30 pm – 2.30 pm – 4.30 pm. From Arguineguín: 11.15 am – 1.15 pm – 3.15 pm – 5 pm. But, just to be sure, double-check the departure times!

HOTELS

Most of the accommodation available here is in apartments or bungalows. The only hotel (three-star) also happens to be one of the best in terms of quality and value for your money:

Hotel Puerto Azul

Enormous double rooms (58 sq m), each with a spacious balcony, panoramic view, separate bedrooms, kitchenette and dining area in the living room. You can opt for self-catering if you prefer. Swimming pool with massage jets, two AstroTurf tennis courts, miniature golf and children's play area. Shuttle bus to the beach (two minutes). *Tel. 56 05 91; Fax 56 14 93; Category (H) 2-3*

BEACHES

Playa de Puerto Rico

This man-made, golden sandy beach is about 400 m long and centrally located in the harbour area. Safe for children with relatively calm and clean water, however, it is often very crowded with young, predominantly English, tourists.

SPORTS & LEISURE

Bowling

There are eight bowling alleys opposite the main entrance to the *La Bolera* shopping centre. Noon–2 pm daily, 400 ptas per game (incl. socks and shoes). 1 game = 10 shots

Deep-sea fishing

There are a number of boats in the harbour that are fully equipped and can be hired for deep-sea fishing expeditions. You don't have to be an experienced fisherman to enjoy this relaxing sport and it makes for a fun day out on the water. Equipment hire is included in the price. Usually between four and a maximum of ten fishermen can be accommodated per boat.

Departure is typically between 8 and 9 am and you get back between 4 and 5 pm. The price is approximately 5,000–8,000 ptas per person. You can also charter the boats and their crews for between 40,000 and 60,000 ptas per diem. Amongst the better-known charter boats are Carmen I, Blue Marlin and the M. Y. Dorado.

Sailing, windsurfing & diving

Puerto Rico is ideal for sailing, windsurfing and scuba diving. The following establishment will cater for all your needs: *Overschmidt Sail and Surf, Helmut Dembski, Puerto Rico (Puerto Base), 1st landing stage (at the end); Tel. and Fax 56 52 92.* The *Top Diving Padi* diving school is located just opposite.

Squash

There are three squash courts right next to the tennis courts: 8 am–10 pm daily, 1,000 ptas per hour plus 200 ptas per racket. No reservations are taken – bookings can only be made on the spot.

Puerto Rico beach can get quite crowded

Tennis
There are four public clay tennis courts near the bus station between the shopping centre and the main street. The cost of a court is 800 ptas per hour or 1,000 ptas with floodlights. Courts are rented on a first come, first serve basis.

Water-ski and jet-ski
Located next to Martín's sailing school, *Escuela de Vela*: about 3,500 ptas for 30 minutes. Instruction available. Jet-ski facilities next to the water tobogan course also at about 3,500 ptas per 30 minutes.

ENTERTAINMENT

There is live music and dancing every night in the *Bahía Playa* restaurant (near the water slide). There is usually a good atmosphere in the large *Centro Comercial* (shopping centre – the Hannenfass is a popular pub there) and in *Oscar's Pub* on the promenade. Young people gather mostly in the various discos and the shopping centre.

INFORMATION

Patronato para la Promoción y el Fomento del Turismo de Mogán
Puerto Rico, in the large shopping centre; Tel. 56 00 29; Fax 56 10 50

SURROUNDING AREA

'La Costa' between Puerto Rico and Puerto de Mogán (104/C4–5)
The coastal road between Puerto Rico and Puerto de Mogán was relaid 25 years ago, though you may come across the occasional bumpy stretch of the old road, the *camino*. It leads through the mountains and runs parallel to the coast where the scenery is wild and picturesque. It can be quite hair-raising in parts, with sharp bends and vertiginous drops!

Playa del Cura (104/C5)
This 400-m-long sandy beach is only a stone's throw from Tauro. It is surrounded by hotel complexes so it tends to get quite crowded. There is accommodation for about 2,500 visitors around the bay. The *Riviera* hotel is right by the water. It was one of the first hotels to be built here and it has maintained its popularity despite increasing competition. *Beach hotel Riviera, Playa del Cura; Tel. 56 09 37; Category (H) 2*

Playa del Medio Almud (104/C5)
⊙ This beach is about 70 m long and quite rocky and slippery in places. The sand is not all that well tended and you have to clamber over many rocks to reach it. It is a popular place amongst the locals

for camping with their whole family, particularly in summer. Consequently, there's a Spanish-Canarian beach party going on practically every day – if you're lucky enough, you may be invited to join one. It might turn out to be your fondest memory of your experiences under the Canarian sun.

Playa de Tiritaña **(104/C4–5)**
This beach is popular amongst independent travellers and can only be reached on foot. The path starts at the road and descends about 600 m down the cliff. The beach itself, situated between imposing cliffs, is rather narrow. The water is wonderfully clean, but beware of strong currents!

Tauro **(104/C4–5)**
Tauro is not a village, or even a hamlet – just a scattered group of houses nestled between two campsites and an aubergine plantation at the entrance to the Tauro Valley. These homes are occupied for the most part by long-term holidaymakers or foreign residents.

The Playa de Tauro is about 400 m long and although it has mostly fine sand, there are a number of stony patches and rocky outcrops here and there. There are a few bars and houses by the beach and you can get a rather good meal at the *Guantánamo* restaurant on the main road *(Category 2/3)*.

SAN AGUSTÍN

(106/B–C5) Along with Maspalomas and Playa des Inglés, San Agustín is one of the largest tourist resorts on the Costa Canaria, undoubtedly the most attractive coastal region of the island. The town is protected from the wind as it nestles in a sheltered hollow surrounded by hills that slope gently down to the sea. The tomato plantations have been replaced by bungalows, apartment blocks and hotels, which cover practically every inch of ground right up to the water's edge. The first impression is not an altogether favourable one – a sea of concrete instead of a sea of blue. But this impression is deceptive in many ways. The town has a number of gardens and green spaces and a pleasant promenade, making San Agustín a much more peaceful place than the neighbouring resort of Playa del Inglés. However, not so peaceful is the four-lane highway that divides San Agustín in two. It would be unwise to try and cross this road – use one of the many pedestrian underpasses. The accommodation on the far side of the road provides a wonderful view of the bay, while those staying nearer the sea can enjoy the lovely promenade along the coast.

RESTAURANTS

Chez Mario
One of the longest-established restaurants in the south offering Italian and Spanish cuisine. *Urbanización Nueva Europa, Aguila Playa, San Agustín; Tel. 76 18 17, 7 pm–1 am daily; Category 2*

Loopy's Tavern
Not exactly the most traditional of Canarian restaurants but something different with its wooden décor and bric-a-brac.

Well-prepared, substantial cuisine. *C/Retama 31, San Agustín; Tel. 76 28 92; 10–1 am; Category 2/3*

HOTEL

Don Gregory

This hotel lies right on the sea front next to a beach ideal for children. All 220 double rooms have a sea view and are well furnished. The hotel was refurbished a few years ago and has its very own bakery as well as a tennis court. *C/Retama; Tel. 77 38 77; Fax 76 99 96; Category (H) 1/2*

SPORTS & LEISURE

The Viajes Maspalomas travel agency organizes walking tours in the mountains for small groups. *Viajes Maspalomas S. A., San Agustín, shopping centre, Unit No. 252; Tel. 76 41 95; Fax 76 42 95; 9 am–1 pm, 4–8 pm Mon–Sat*

BEACHES

The Playa de San Agustín is one of the best-tended and most popular beaches on the island, about 2 km long and up to 80 m wide. It has fine golden sand, which is broken up by natural rock barriers that act as protection against excessive swells. If you're here early enough, you can sometimes watch the local fishermen hauling in the day's catch.

ENTERTAINMENT

Casino

Those who wish to try their luck after an exhausting day on the beach can visit the Casino Gran Canaria. The atmosphere is elegant but casual, however, if you turn up in shorts or beachwear, you won't be admitted. Don't forget your passport! *C/Retama 4; Tel. 76 27 24; 9 pm–4 am daily; Admission: 500 ptas*

Cabaret

The cabaret-restaurant *Casino Palace*, next to the casino, offers a range of entertainment, from floor shows to dancing. *Playa de San Agustín; Tel. 76 68 28 or 76 68 34; Admission including meal: from 6,500 ptas per person; Advance booking required!*

SURROUNDING AREA

Juan Grande (107/D4)

Juan Grande is a small village on the road between San Agustín and Vecindario. The aristocratic 'de la Vega Grande de Guadalupe del Castillo y Bravo de Laguna' family have their estate here, which is an oasis of greenery in an arid landscape.

The fishing village of *Castillo del Romeral* is only a short distance away. The beach here is lined with dozens of boats, but looks more like a quarry than anything else. The fishermen's co-operative, the *Cofradía de pescadores*, serves a wide selection of tasty *tapas.*

Playa del Aguila (106/C5)

This narrow, some 400-m-long beach lies at the mouth of the 'Eagle Gorge' ('aguila' means eagle), 2 km north of San Agustín. The sand is golden brown with rocky patches. The water is relatively clean, though layers of algae appear periodically on the surface.

Sioux City (106/C5)

This 'Wild West Town', north-east of San Agustín, is a great place for children. A reconstructed cowboy town, complete with saloon, bank, church, prison and its very own Boot Hill looks just like we know it from Westerns. The Saloon Theatre's repertoire includes a variety of shows and demonstrations: mock gunfights, lassoing, shooting, horse-riding and open-air parodies of Westerns. *Cañon del Aguila; Tel. 76 29 82; 10 am–8 pm daily except Mon; shows every hour; Admission: 2,000 ptas (adults), 1,000 ptas (children); Barbecue on Fri, with open bar and live country music; Admission: 5,000 ptas (adults), 2,500 ptas (children)*

SAN BARTOLOMÉ DE TIRAJANA

(**106/B2**) Old Canarians still call this pretty mountain town 'queer', as it was called in pre-Hispanic times. But don't think that it's just a quaint and dreamy little place. San Bartolomé de Tirajana, a former shepherds' settlement, which for centuries was a sleepy village 28 km from Playa del Inglés, today is a community that has undergone major development and tourism and has become prosperous in the process. According to cautious estimates by a major travel agency, the lovely place has had annual revenues of about 170 thousand million ptas since 1984. Consequently, the population of this area has vastly increased. Today, it is the administrative centre for many of the surrounding tourist resorts on the Costa Canaria from Bahía Feliz via San Agustín to far beyond the Maspalomas Oasis.

SIGHTS

Wash-house

When you consider that Tirajana has become the largest tourist centre in all of Spain, the fact that the old wash-house diagonally opposite the church is still in working order lends a certain charm to the place. The water is chanelled into a stone trough from an underground source and you can still see women doing the family wash here from time to time.

HOTEL

Finca El Oso

Twelve comfortable rooms in a charming converted farmhouse right by the *Presa de Chira* reservoir (about 30 minutes by car from Tirajana), for lovers of nature and sports. Electricity, showers, toilets, swimming pool, sauna, pool billiard, ping pong, terrace bar with barbecue and buffet. The chef and owner has tried for years to obtain a hotel licence. Since he still hasn't been successful, you must become a club member to stay overnight. Canoes, fishing equipment and deckchairs can be hired. The chef, El Oso ('the Bear'), will also be glad to give you information on additional overnight accommodation in less accessible parts (*turismo rural*) of the island. *Presa de Chira; Tel. 12 90 04; Fax 12 90 46; club members pay 3,000 ptas per night half-board*

SURROUNDING AREA

Caldera Tirajana (**106/A-C1-2**)

San Bartolomé de Tirajana is at the centre of a vast fruit-growing area on the edge of the fertile and geologically facinating *Caldera de Tirajana.* 'Caldera' is Spanish for cauldron. The backdrop to the Tirajana Cauldron is formed by an imposing rock face over which the highest mountain on the island, Pozo de las Nieves, towers. This mountain can be easily identified by the two bright white semicircular transmitters and radar station – part of the island's air defence network – on its peak.

Some of the best walks from Tirajana are in the *Pilancones* nature reserve, where you can visit the 'pine caves', *Las Cuevas del Pinar*, or the 'white caves', *Las Cuevas Blancas,* before the 1,200-m-high Cruz-Grande Ridge, on the way to Ayacata, where the Chapel of Santiago (La Ermita de Santiago) is located. You can also make your way to the *Presa de Chira* reservoir, a popular destination, especially for those with a jeep, because of the spectacular scenery that surrounds it.

SAN NICOLÁS DE TOLENTINO

(**100/B5**) San Nicolás de Tolentino lies 5 km from the sea, in a fertile valley. The locals refer to this place in the far west of the island simply as *Aldea,* or 'village', though San Nicolás could hardly be classified as a village today. It's a thriving, bustling town of about 11,000 inhabitants and a prosperous place, thanks to the fertile land that surrounds it.

Hiking in Gran Canaria is an experience not to be missed

RESTAURANTS & HOTELS

Segundo

Restaurant, bar and guest house in a central location. Basic cuisine, seven small double rooms. *C/Alfonso XIII, no. 14; Tel. 89 11 65 or 89 09 01; Category 3.* A hotel has recently been annexed to the establishment: *Los Cascajos; 20 clean double rooms; Category (H) 3.*

There is a nice little fishing village at the mouth of the valley, which is worth a visit if you like fresh fish. *Puerto de la Aldea* remains largely unspoilt and has a number of good restaurants (some more touristy than others), where you can have a freshly prepared fish meal, usually for a reasonable price.

BEACHES

Playa de San Nicolás

This steep and stony beach is about 500 m long. Here, you'll find a promenade, a small pine wood, a lagoon (not always filled with water) and a picnic area. One of the better places to sit and watch the sunset.

SURROUNDING AREA

Road to Artenara (100-101/B-E4-5)

From San Nicolás you can take the winding, steep and spectacular road to Artenara, the highest settlement on the island. The trip will leave you with a lasting memory as you travel through a landscape that time has forgotten on a road reminiscent of the trip from Aldea to Agaete – the C 810, the highway that goes right around the island, cutting through rock faces 400 to 600 m above sea level. When the weather is nice, you can see Tenerife and the Pico de Teide. This road shows the island both at its most spectacular and its most dangerous. It is recommended only for those who have a head for heights because the sheer drops can be quite terrifying. You have to drive very carefully as you may come across a recent rockfall blocking the way, so take the bends slowly and with caution. The road is closed in wet weather.

SANTA LUCÍA

(106/C2) If you want to get some idea of what life must have been like on the island before the onset of mass tourism, then a trip to Santa Lucía will satisfy your curiosity. Several small hamlets, including *Risco del Cuervo, Sorrueda, Casas Blancas* and others are spread out overlooking the wonderful landscape of the valley around Santa Lucía de Tirajana. They have only recently become accessible by car and there are still a good number of them that can be reached only on foot or by donkey.

This is where you'll find the typical Canarian farmhouses or *casas terreras.* These simple buildings consist of two or three rooms under a thick-beamed roof with an inner courtyard. They are generally crammed full of farming equipment and have the token cage with canary. Each kitchen has its own *pila,* or filter, for water purification and a stove as a separate, cube-shaped entity.

The little village of Santa Lucía itself is quite African, or rather Berber-like, in appearance. Its church dome is impressive.

MUSEUM

Museo del Castillo

Opposite the tiny *Hao Bar* ('hao' is a greeting in Canarian dialect), you'll find a museum, known officially as the *Museo del Castillo de la Fortaleza* – Museum of the Castle Fortress. The former mayor of Santa Lucía came up with the idea and the funding for this project to house the collection of archaeological finds that he had carefully gathered over a period of some 40 years. Today, this collection is lovingly displayed here in the museum. *C/Los Alamos; 9 am–7 pm daily; Admission: 300 ptas*

RESTAURANT

Hao

★ The atmosphere and cuisine are typically Canarian. The tables and chairs are made from massive eucalyptus and palm trunks, and the shade-giving roof from *caña.* The view of the 'market garden', with its apricot, lemon and orange trees, is lovely and the smooth, local red wine (*vino tinto*) goes perfectly with the surroundings. *C/Los Alamos; Tel. 79 80 07; 9 am–7 pm daily; Category 3*

TELDE

(**103/E5**) This town, with a population of 80,000, is the second-largest on Gran Canaria and its suburbs stretch almost as far as the airport. If you are approaching it from the airport, one of the first things you will see on your left as you head for Las Palmas is a Canary Island Colosseum – the ruins of a bull-fighting arena, the *Plaza de Toros.* The reason the place is in ruins is simple: despite their Spanish heritage, the islanders are not crazy about full-fighting. Several one-way streets lead into Telde's bustling centre with the vivacious old town.

SIGHTS

Barrio San Francisco

There are a number of fascinating old buildings tucked away in the labyrinthine alleys and narrow streets of the old town. One can clearly tell that their owners are wealthy. Telde used to be significant as a place where slaves brought over from Africa to work the sugar plantations were housed.

Iglesia de San Juan Bautista

The parish church of San Juan Bautista (John the Baptist) dates from the late 15th century. Built from volcanic stone, the design is largely Spanish-influenced. There is a portal that is almost purely Gothic in style. The church is amongst the oldest on the island and it houses some of the greatest art treasures on Gran Canaria, most notably the carved wooden main altar. This piece, over 2 m high, was brought all the way from Flanders and is more than 500 years old. The statue of Christ, which came from Mexico, is also worth a closer look.

MUSEUM

Museo León y Castillo

Fernando de León y Castillo, the Spanish diplomat and politician, and his brother Juan, an engineer, were born in Telde. Juan gained renown towards the end of the last century through the creation of the harbour in Las Palmas as well as numerous streets, including today's motorway. The house the two brothers were born in is now a little museum with displays that illustrate how the other half lived. *Calle León y Castillo 45; 8 am–3 pm Mon–Fri; Admission free*

RESTAURANTS

La Alameda

There is always something going on in one or the other of Telde's bars. One of the best is the simple *tapas* bar *La Alameda. C/Juan Carlos I, in the Plaza San Juan; 9 am–11 pm daily; Category 3*

Restaurant-Grill Silva

A popular restaurant, three minutes' drive from the airport. *Carretera General del Goro 1; Tel. 69 74 55; 12 noon–12 midnight daily; Category 3*

SHOPPING

You can find all sorts of shops in the main street, the *Calle León y Castillo*, in the centre of town and several side streets. There are bars, cafés, banks, shoe shops, fabric shops, stores for dishes and electric appliances, hardware stores as well as householdware shops. Service is usually very friendly. Sometimes shop owners are even willing to haggle and will lower their prices for their customers.

HOTEL

Hotel Bahía Mar

The only hotel in Telde is 6 km away from the old town, on the beach at *La Estrella.* It is luxurious and modern with an old-fashioned style. Seventy-two double rooms, sea views, swimming pool and fine décor. *Urbanización La Estrella – La Garita – Telde; Tel. 69 16 41/44; Fax 69 69 64; Category 2*

BEACHES

You'll find several relatively small beaches in the coastal areas around *La Estrella, La Garita, Melenara, Las Salinetas* and *Ojo de Garza.* The locals and hobby anglers prefer the beaches that slope deeply into the water. A word of caution – because of the north-westerly winds, the swells tend to be quite strong and the currents can be dangerous.

ENTERTAINMENT

Sala de Baile

A well-known *sala de fiesta* or *sala de baile* – a place where you can dance the night away on Fridays and Saturdays – is directly by the motorway *(Restaurante Mi Niño, 13 km from Las Palmas). 7 pm–12 midnight Mon–Thurs, 7 pm–4 am Fri and Sat, closed Sun; Tel. 69 66 02*

INFORMATION

Concejalía de Turismo

Plaza de San Juan 1; 8 am–3 pm Mon–Fri; Tel. 69 57 83 (employees have only rudimentary knowledge of foreign languages)

SURROUNDING AREA

The Coast **(103/F5–6)**

The stretch of coast immediately below Telde beyond the motorway isn't exactly inviting and not to everyone's taste. Still, there are a couple of places in the steppe-like landscape of banana and tomato plantations, amongst the scree, dumps of cinder and various businesses, that are quite appealing. The quality of the water, however, is not consistently high.

Valsequillo **(102/C5)**
Valsequillo (pop. 7,000) has been blessed with an accommodating climate. The land is under intensive agriculture, especially in the upper reaches of the *Barranco de San Miguel*. The neighbouring valley, *Valle de San Roque*, is famous for its mineral water, which is considered by many to be the best on the island. It certainly has the highest mineral content and is particularly rich in magnesium, calcium, fluoride and sulphur.

Due to its sheltered location, Valsequillo can become unbearably hot in the summer months. As a result, some of the fields are cultivated using dry-farming techniques. You can get a great view over the surrounding countryside from the *Montaña de El Helechal*, which reaches a height of 765 m. The mountain is about 2 km away from Valsequillo itself.

VECINDARIO

(107/D-E3-4) Since 1970, Vecindario has had to accommodate a population growth of over 1,000 per cent. The once sleepy village, halfway between the airport and San Agustín, has turned into a lively, bustling little town overnight. The cause of this rapid expansion was, of course, tourism. The tomato plantations on which the villagers once depended for their income were becoming economically unviable, and the land was turned over to the builders. Unfortunately, growth has been so rapid that there has been no time to develop an adequate infrastructure. Most of the 25,000 inhabitants are employed in tourist-related service industries on the nearby Costa Canaria, mostly as cooks, waiters, plumbers, porters, chambermaids and administrators. Consequently, Vecindario has enveloped the neighbouring villages of *El Doctoral*, *Sardina* and *Cruce de Sardina*.

HOTEL

Hostal Residencia Paco
Fifteen simple double rooms with sinks. *Avda Canarias 278 (main street); Tel. 75 34 52; Category (G) 1/2*

SHOPPING

You'll find one shop after another all along the former 'tomato road' (parallel to the motorway). People from the surrounding areas who don't want to go all the way to Las Palmas consider Vecindario to be *the* place to shop. The variety of businesses that have sprung up in recent years is indeed astounding: there are car dealers, furniture and clothing stores, supermarkets, specialized shops – in short, you'll find anything you want.

If you're looking to buy some local flowers or cacti, try the *viveros*, the Canarian equivalent to a garden centre.

SURROUNDING AREA

Pozo Izquierdo **(107/E4)**
To the south of the town, you'll find a narrow road branching off to the sea. It leads down to the area known as Pozo Izquierdo, which has become famous as a training camp for expert and professional windsurfers, thanks to the strong winds that whip along the coast. Since 1993, world championships have been held here.

Waves, woods and volcanoes

These routes are marked in green on the map on the inside front cover and in the Road Atlas beginning on page 99

① A TRIP AROUND THE MINIATURE CONTINENT

The perimeter of the island, which is almost perfectly round, is 250 km long. It has many different landscapes, unique flora and different climatic zones directly bordering on one another. Circumnavigating the island along its fascinating coast, through stone deserts, jagged mountains, fertile valleys and romantic fishing villages, takes a whole day. It is a trip that will give you an impression of the entire archipelago and will probably make you want to venture on additional outings, for many of the places are well worth a second visit. Theoretically, the trip around the island by car could be accomplished in about three hours without taking a break, but four to five hours of driving time is a more realistic estimate.

From *Playa del Inglés (pp. 69–72)* you take the motorway to Mogán. The coastal road 810 begins at Arguineguín. It leaves the south's arid, rocky coast near Puerto de Mogán and leads you into the exquisite landscape of the *Barranco de Mogán*. However, first you can stop over in *Puerto de Mogán (pp. 73–76)*, where you can convince yourself that the island's south has more to offer than faceless fortresses made mostly of beds. Even though the epithet 'Little Venice' is an exaggeration, nowhere on the entire island will you find a more harmonious blend of tourism and nature than in the romantic bungalow settlement of Puerto de Mogán with its canals, its profusion of beautiful flowers and impressive marina. Continuing on towards the village of *Mogán (pp. 68)*, which is 250 m above sea level, you can enjoy the beauty of palm trees, the luxuriance of blossoms, agaves, prickly-pear cacti and pine trees in a wild and romantic mountain landscape. Mogán is ideal as the starting point for hikes in this area.

Right after you leave the village you can take the road to Ayacata. At first it is covered with asphalt, yet soon it turns into a rather adventurous gravel track, but don't worry: your car will manage quite well. We recommend that you take side trips to the reservoir lakes *Presa de las Niñas* with a capacity of five million cubic metres of water or the smaller *Presa del Mulato*, which is only three kilometres further east. If you have good hiking equipment, you can climb the island's mountain peaks from here, but be sure that you are in good shape!

To continue your trip, you follow the mountain road GC 810, which winds its way up the mountain ridge in the west. You will pass the *Barranco de Veneguera*, at whose entrance is a lonely rocky beach. After approximately four kilometres you will see the famous many-coloured rock faces of *Los Azulejos*. As their name indicates, viewers with some imagination may be reminded of painted tiles. The lack of colours in the flora of this region is made up for by the gorgeous colours of the various layers of volcanic stone. Only here and there will you see mostly endemic flowers, such as the tabaiba. On the mountain peaks are the coniferous forests of Tamadaba. Now you are crossing the *Barranco de Tasarte* and after just a few kilometres, you will reach the mountain pass *Degollada de Tasartico* (576 m). Suddenly, Gran Canaria's largest valley, the *Aldea*, is in full view. Passing greenhouses and plantations, you go down the winding road towards *San Nicolás de Tolentino (pp. 84-85)*. If you want to see *Puerto de la Aldea* – a sleepy port today – turn left just after exiting San Nicolás.

From San Nicolás on you almost never lose sight of the sea as you go along the steep coast at several hundred metres above sea level. After about three kilometres, a street sign picturing a camera indicates the *Mirador del Balcón*, a magnificent lookout point. From this balcony-like viewpoint at 400 m above sea level, you can see the island's entire west coast. You continue your trip by passing the small village of *El Risco*. Gradually, the coastal road approaches sea level again.

In the distance, the white houses of *Puerto de las Nieves* appear, the port of *Agaete (pp. 34-36)*. A stroll to the picturesque harbour to the old mole to take a photograph from there of the basalt monolith *Dedo de Dios*, the 'finger of God', is a must. Even though the new harbour connecting Agaete with Tenerife detracts somewhat from some of the fishing village's romantic air, it has managed to retain its charm. If the *Ermita de las Nieves* is open, don't fail to take a look into this beautiful chapel with its woodcuts depicting the Virgin Mary! We also recommend visiting the restaurant *Las Nasas (C/Nuestra Senora de las Nieves s/n; 11 am–10 pm daily; No tel., Category 2/3)*.

For a cup of coffee after lunch, you should visit the *Hotel Guyarmina* at the end of the Agaete Valley, the perhaps most fertile area on the entire island. From behind the square by the church *Iglesia de Concepción* you go towards Las Palmas for about one kilometre, and when you see the sign saying *Al Valle*, you turn right. This beautiful valley is really worth visiting for a whole day, but for now you'll want to continue on route GC 810 towards Gáldar. Shortly before you have reached the village of *San Isidro*, a sign saying *Reptilandia (p. 38)* invites you to make a left turn and view more than one hundred different animal species in well-kept open-air enclosures.

A short while later, even before you have reached Gáldar, you can take another side trip you will find well worth your while. To reach *Sardina del Norte (p. 48)*, you turn left, and after just a few kilometres, passing banana plantations, you will reach a little port. If you go all the way to the end of it, you will reach the excellent restaurant *La Fragata*. Should you decide to forego this little excursion, you will immediately reach the royal town of *Gáldar (pp. 37–38)*. Don't be shocked: the place is rather unsightly, but walking through the old part of town to the church *Iglesia Santiago de los Caballeros* will not disappoint you!

You won't have far to go from Gáldar to the 'cheese town' of *Guía*. Soon after you exit the town, there is another almost obligatory detour: if you turn right, you will go towards the *Cenobio de Valerón (p. 48)*, the famous cave dwellings of the island's original inhabitants. However, you will then miss the ride across Gran Canaria's 128-m-high bridge over the *Barranco de Silva*. At the end of this bridge, you have yet another breathtaking view of a fascinating part of the island. Continuing your trip on the urban motorway, you pass several towns right by the coast: the very pretty *San Felipe (p. 48)*, *San Andrés, El Roque* and *Quintanilla*. Here, by the roadside, is where you'll find *Mesón Grill Atlántico (12 noon – 12 midnight Tues–Sun; Tel. 62 67 89; Category 2/3)*, a restaurant with excellent yet inexpensive food. At the Costa de Bañaderos the surf is especially fierce. Even strong and experienced swimmers are strongly urged to refrain from testing the waters here!

Continuing on in the direction of Las Palmas, you reach the *Punta de Arucas*, from where you can enjoy a panoramic view of the entire capital. You can stay on the urban motorway and before you reach the roundabout outside Las Palmas, you will enter an underpass. Going straight ahead again, get onto the coastal road, where you turn right in the direction of *Aeropuerto/Sur*, the motorway that brings you back to Playa del Inglés.

② INTO THE FERTILE HEART OF THE ISLAND AND ITS BREATHTAKING ALPINE SCENERY

As beautiful and enjoyable as the sun and the beach are, at some point you might hear the call of the mountains. Follow this call to Gran Canaria's mountains, which are almost 2,000 m high, contain a spectacular and a unique world that is reminiscent of various parts of Central or South-eastern Europe and, in others, resembles a bizarre moonscape. The trip starting in Playa del Inglés is 180 km long, which will take approximately four hours of actual driving time, but you'll want to stop in so many different places to discover the beauties of Gran Canaria that you should probably schedule an entire day for this excursion. Don't forget to bring along proper clothes: if the temperature near the coast is 28°C, it might be a relatively crisp 10°C in the mountains.

Whichever road you take, you'll end up at the Cruz de Tejeda, at 1,450 m above sea level, Gran Canaria's highest pass. Though you can take the motorway from Playa del Inglés, the 'classic', fastest and most convenient route starts in Las Palmas and leads via the GC 811 through the suburb of *Tafira (pp. 48-50)*. It is a rather wealthy place with one villa after the other, but *Monte Lentiscal*, which borders it directly, is even wealthier. Eucalyptus trees skirt the street, which has now widened to two lanes. We recommend that you take a left at the gas station and follow the signs saying *Caldera de Bandama* to get a view of the volcanic crater and the nearby golf course.

Back on the main street, the trip continues up into the island's fertile interior and agricultural centre. Amongst the numerous towns and villages scattered throughout this area are *Santa Brígida (pp. 46–47)* with an old town at its centre well worth a visit and, a few kilometres farther up, *San Mateo (pp. 27 and 33)*, the island's most important market place. A visit in the market hall to the left of the main street, behind the bus terminal, will quickly convince you how superior the quality of the local agriculture is, and perhaps you'll even feel inspired to do some shopping here for a picnic in the mountains! Almost all restaurants in this area offer good food, though meat must naturally be more recommended here than fish. The cheese stands comparison to the dairy products from Guía. After a visit at the museum restaurant *Casa de Cho Zacarías (p. 51)*, you've almost become an expert in rural life.

Above San Mateo, there are fewer and fewer houses as you approach actual wilderness. After passing the village of *La Lechuza*, watch for the restaurant *Las Rosas* to the left of the street so you won't miss the small junction to *Cueva Grande*, a small mountain village. A sign tells you that you are about to enter a nature reserve. Right above Cueva Grande begins the mixed forest and soon you'll be in pine woods. At an intersection, you should keep to the right and go in the direction of Cruz de Tejeda, passing lookout points offering spellbinding panoramic views of Gran Canaria's landmark, the monolith *Roque Nublo*, and *Roque Bentaiga (p. 59)*, the monumental sacrificial site in the collapsed crater.

You have the best view of the volcanic landscape and all the way to Tenerife from the terrace of the restaurant *Cruz de Tejeda (p. 57)* of the Parador chain. The picturesque village of *Tejeda (pp. 57–58)* is only 5 km further downhill, in the direction of Ayacata. It is already 400 m closer to sea level, embedded in almond trees whose fruits are sold at the Parador. From the hotel, you should follow the GC 811, which leads to Las Palmas. Ignoring the street turning to Valleseco after 2 km, you will pass the mountain village of *Las Lagunetas (p. 51)* after about 5 km. The street is now lined with chestnut trees. Often, the *Barranco de las Minas* at your right and the *Barranco de las Lagunetas* at your left contain water, and the terraced fields give you an idea of how fertile this region is. Soon you get to the junction to Cueva Grande and reach *San Mateo*. You now turn right onto the GC 815 leading towards Valsequillo and enter the historic town of *Telde (pp. 86-87)*, where after so much nature you can now also dip into some culture. You then take the motorway from Telde to get to *Playa del Inglés (pp. 69–72)*, which is only 20 minutes' drive away. If you have still some time left, you may want to take the country road running parallel to the motorway to pass through the villages of *Ingenio (p. 65)* and *Agüimes (p. 65)*, where you can hunt for arts-and-crafts items.

Practical information

Important addresses and useful information for your visit to Gran Canaria

AMERICAN & BRITISH ENGLISH

The Marco Polo travel guides are written in British English. In North America, certain terms and usages deviate from British usage. Some of the more frequently encountered examples are:
baggage for luggage, billion for milliard, cab for taxi, car rental for car hire, drugstore for chemist's, fall for autumn, first floor for groundfloor, freeway/highway for motorway, gas(oline) for petrol, railroad for railway, restroom for toilet/lavatory, streetcar for tram, subway for underground/tube, toll-free numbers for freephone numbers, trailer for caravan, trunk for boot, vacation for holidays, wait staff for waiting staff (in restaurants etc.), zip code for postal code.

BUSES

All towns and most villages can be reached relatively easily by public transport. The bus network is particularly well structured in the more touristic south, and buses are so frequent, it is impossible to give the entire schedule here. Information on times and routes can be obtained directly from the central bus station in Las Palmas or from the tourist information office in the *Yumbo* shopping centre in Playa del Inglés (above the Banco de Bilbao and Banco Central; most employees speak at least broken English). This *Oficina de Salcai* has up-to-date bus timetables and sells tickets at reduced prices (*Tel. 76 53 32; Fax 76 53 59*).

CAMPING

Camping – including putting up your RV – is usually tolerated wherever it isn't expressly prohibited. Gran Canaria also has one large campsite: *El Camping Guantánamo*, on the Puerto Rico–Mogán road. *Tel. 56 20 98; Fax 56 07 66; Open all year round*

CAR HIRE

The cost of car hire on Gran Canaria is relatively reasonable. The following companies usually offer a good choice of vehicles:

Las Palmas *Autos Hertz, C/Sagasta 27; Tel. 26 45 76*

Airport (arrivals hall) all major car hire services

San Agustín *Avis, Carretera General; Tel. 76 14 54*

Playa del Inglés *Autos Orlando, Avda Tirajana; Tel. 76 24 85*

CONSULATES

Britain:
Edificio Cataluña,
Calle des Luis Morote 6
Las Palmas
Tel. (928) 26 25 08

United States:
Calle José Franchy Roca 5
Las Palmas
Tel. (928) 27 12 59

CUSTOMS

In terms of customs law, Gran Canaria is considered a 'third country'. This translates into the following restrictions: no more than 2 l wine or 1 l of liquor may be taken off the island without a customs charge. The limit for tobacco is 200 cigarettes or 100 cigarillos or 50 cigars.

A typical road in the central massif

DOCTORS

We strongly recommend that you take out a private medical insurance to cover you for the duration of your stay.

EMERGENCIES

Police: *Tel. 0 91 or 0 92*

GETTING TO THE OTHER ISLANDS

Any travel agency *(agencia de viajes)* will gladly give you details on how to get to the other Canary Islands by boat or plane.

INFORMATION

Useful information for your holiday can be obtained from the Spanish National Tourist Office:

Britain:
57–58 St James's Street
London SW1A 1LD
Tel. (0171) 499 0901

United States:
665 Fifth Avenue
New York, NY 10022
Tel. (212) 759-8822

Gran Canaria:
Casa del Turismo
Parque Santa Catalina
Las Palmas
Tel. (928) 26 23 55

Canarian Tourist Office:
Patronato de Tourismo
C/Leon y Castillo 17
Las Palmas de Gran Canaria
Tel. 36 24 22 or 36 22 22 or 36 26 22, Fax 36 28 22

MEASURES & WEIGHTS

1 cm	0.39 inch
1 m	1.09 yd (3.28 ft)
1 km	0.62 miles
1 m²	1.20 yd²
1 ha	2.47 acres
1 km²	0.39 mi²
1 g	0.035 ounces
1 kg	2.21 pounds
British ton	*1016 kg*
US ton	*907 kg*

1 l itre is equivalent to 0.22 Imperial gallons and 0.26 US gallons

MONEY

You can cash Eurocheques in Spain up to a maximum of 25,000 ptas. If you have a British post office account you can draw money from any Spanish post office free of charge. More and more banks have cash-dispensing machines that accept EC and other major credit cards.

NUDE BATHING

Nude bathing is tolerated by the authorities on the middle section of Playa de Maspalomas. Topless bathing is common and permitted on any beach.

PASSPORTS & VISAS

EU nationals must carry a valid passport or identity card. Children under 16 should either be entered on a parent's passport or have their own. American and Canadian visitors don't need a visa, but Australian nationals will need to apply for one from the Spanish consulate. Cats and dogs will need an official certificate testifying that they have been vaccinated against rabies.

PETROL STATIONS

Opening times: from around 6 am to 9 pm Mon–Sat, closed on Sundays and holidays, but around 20 petrol stations remain on standby until 2 pm. The following petrol stations stay open all day on Sundays and bank holidays: CEPSA in Fataga and MOBIL in Puerto de Mogán. You can purchase butane gas from DISA and CEPSA gas stations. A 13-kg bottle *(bombona)* costs 1,107 ptas. *All empty bottles must be returned*

POST (CORREO)

The post offices (*oficinas de correo*) are open Mon–Sat from about 6 am to 9 pm and closed on Sundays and holidays. These times vary at some places. In Las Palmas, a number of post office windows are also staffed from 4 to 6 pm. Here are the addresses of post offices from where you can send faxes and telegrams, and make or receive telegraphic money transfers (telégrafos 8 am–8 pm) weekdays:

Playa del Inglés, *Avda de Tirajana (Ed. Mercurio); Tel. 76 23 41*

Las Palmas central post office, *Avda 1. de Mayo 62; Tel. 36 21 15*

TELEPHONES

Making phone calls is cheapest from a public telephone booth (*cabina de teléfono*, light blue). You can obtain phone cards for 1,000 and 2,000 ptas at phone card dispensing machines, newspaper stands and in some tobacco shops. They work with almost all public telephones. Hotels and special telephone shops tend to add considerable surcharges!

International calls: dial 07 first. After the dial tone, dial the country code (United Kingdom 44, United States and Canada 1, Ireland 353), than the area code without 0 and the desired phone number. To call Gran Canaria from abroad, dial the international code (00 from the UK) followed by the country code, 34, then the area code (e.g., 28 for Las Palmas; if you are phoning Las Palmas from elsewhere on the island the area code is 928).

WHEN TO GO

The climate is favourable all year round. Daytime temperatures can get very hot from July to October. The nights are cooler between December and April.
The sea is at an optimum temperature around September and October. For holiday on the beach, the best time is in the second half of the year, while the first half is better if you wish to pursue various sports.

WEATHER IN LAS PALMAS

Seasonal averages

	Jan	Feb	Mar	Apr	May	June	July	Aug	Sept	Oct	Nov	Dec
Daytime temperatures in °C/F	21/70	22/72	22/72	22/72	23/73	24/75	25/77	25/77	26/79	28/82	24/75	22/72
Night-time temperatures in °C/F	14/57	14/57	15/59	16/61	17/63	18/64	19/66	21/70	21/70	19/66	18/64	16/61
Sunshine: hours per day	6	6	7	8	9	9	9	9	8	7	6	5
Rainfall: days per month	6	3	3	2	1	1	1	1	1	4	6	6
Ocean temperatures in °C/F	19/66	18/64	18/64	18/64	19/66	20/68	21/70	22/72	23/73	23/73	21/70	20/68

Do's and don'ts

How to avoid some of the traps and pitfalls that may face the unwary traveller

Wine

Many organized excursions will take you to places selling so-called Canarian wine, but usually what you're paying good money for is really cheap, inferior wine from mainland Spain.

Restaurants

A number of restaurants in the tourist can only be described as a rip-off. They lure people in by offering meals at ridiculously low prices and then when you're seated, the food served usually matches the price – it's cheap but horrible. In addition, while the food is cheap, any drinks you order with your meal will cost you a fortune.

Time sharing

Instead of buying an apartment or villa outright, with 'time sharing', you buy the right to use the property for a specified period of time – a week, two weeks or three weeks a year.

This method of property dealing is the subject of much controversy. Its legal status in Spain is far from clear and shady time-sharing companies that take the money and run are unfortunately commonplace. Many an unwary tourist has fallen into a time-sharing trap. It's up to you, of course, but you would be strongly advised not to get involved in this sort of business if approached on the streets of your resort. This doesn't mean that all time-share operators are con artists. If you do find the idea appealing, then seek proper legal advice and make sure you use a reputable real estate company instead of one of the more dubious outfits.

Real estate

Amongst the dozens and dozens of real estate agents operating on Gran Canaria, there are certainly a good number of reputable dealers and serious businessmen. But, unfortunately there are also so many sharks that it's extremely difficult to weed them out. The worst crooks tend to target tourists in the hope that the holiday atmosphere will adversely affect their judgement. Let's face it, on holiday, you're more carefree, the wine often flows freely and you may well think to yourself, 'Wouldn't it be great to live here for ever?' As with time shares, it's best to look at things in the cold light of day and not to make any firm decisions while you're actually on holiday. Always seek sound professional advice if you're looking to buy property abroad – word of mouth is as good a method as any for finding reputable dealers. Speak to as many people as you can who have already bought property here.

Shopping

Whether you're on your way to the beach, in a shopping centre or in the street, you'll come across flyers and brochures offering fantastic free coach trips to various destinations. These offers all sound too good to be true, and that's what they tend to be – simply another con. Once on the bus, you get ferried out to some out-of-the-way *finca* or restaurant where the organizers will then try to sell you all kinds of things: blankets and rugs, copper bracelets, magnetic field desensitizers, magic pots… Meanwhile, you're chomping your way through an often indigestible meal where the only good news is that the drinks, and sometimes the food as well, are free.

Excursions

Hire cars cost only half the price they do in Central Europe, but sometimes they're twice as old. Stop signs tell you to yield to other cars, but are frequently ignored. Many cars have brake lights that no longer work. Rear-view mirrors, too, are often considered unnecessary add-ons. The left signal, on the other hand, is absolutely indispensable, as it is more prone to indicate a crash-halt than the driver's intention to turn left.

Generally speaking, weekdays are better for excursions than weekends, when the Canarians are fond of going on trips themselves. Often, there are traffic jams on weekends, and places such as Cruz de Tejeda, Teror or Agaete tend to be overcrowded.

Don't forget that distances, expressed in kilometres don't tell you much about actual travelling time. Advancing 10 km in the mountains can take longer than covering 100 km on a motorway.

If you want to go to Las Palmas from Playa del Inglés, you should take the bus, as in the capital, traffic is horrendous and it can prove difficult to find a parking space. In Las Palmas itself, we recommend that you take taxi cabs.

Colourful billboards in Playa del Inglés

Road Atlas of Gran Canaria

Please refer to back cover for an overview of this Road Atlas

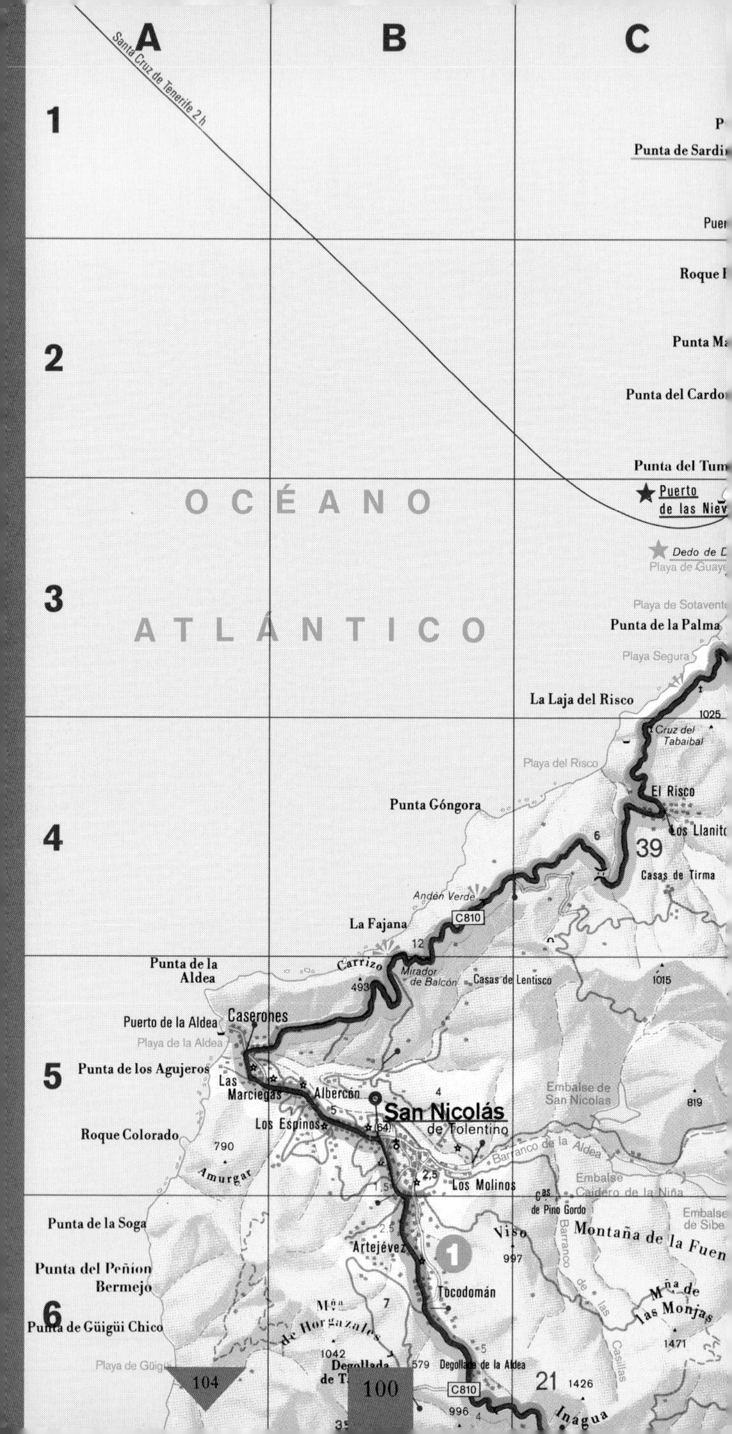
A
B
C
1
2
3
4
5
6
Santa Cruz de Tenerife 2 h
Punta de Sardi
Roque
Punta Ma
Punta del Cardo
Punta del Tum
Puerto de las Niev
Dedo de D
Playa de Guaye
Playa de Sotavent
OCÉANO
ATLÁNTICO
Punta de la Palma
Playa Segura
La Laja del Risco
1025
Cruz del Tabaibal
Playa del Risco
El Risco
Punta Góngora
Los Llanito
39
Casas de Tirma
Andén Verde
C810
La Fajana
12
Punta de la Aldea
Carrizo
Mirador de Balcón
Casas de Lentisco
1015
493
Puerto de la Aldea
Caserones
Playa de la Aldea
Punta de los Agujeros
Las Marciegas
Albercón
Embalse de San Nicolas
819
San Nicolás de Tolentino
Los Espinos
(64)
Roque Colorado
790
Amurga
Barranco de la Aldea
Los Molinos
Embalse Caidero de la Niña
Cas de Pino Gordo
Embalse de Sibe
Punta de la Soga
Viso
Montaña de la Fuen
Artejévez
997
Punta del Peñon Bermejo
Tocodomán
Mña de las Monjas
Punta de Güigüi Chico
Mña de Horgazales
1471
Playa de Güigü
1042
Degollada de T
579
Degollada de la Aldea
21
1426
C810
996
Inagua
104
100

D
E
F
1
Punta de Guanarteme
Punta de Gáldar
Playa de Guanarteme
Puerto Nuevo
Peñas
Punta de la Caleta
El Sobradillo
Punta del Moreno
La Guancha (Nekrópole)
El Agujero
Matas Blancas
Los Llanos
Sta. Elena
Punta del Mármol
Punta Gallegos
Punta de Moya
Pico de Gáldar
434
La Atalaya
GC140
Sardina
5,5
Iglesia
El Burrero
(143)
Cañizares
Playa San Felipe
El Arco
San Felipe
El Roque
Llanos de Botija
Barrial
Gáldar
Cueva Pintada
(186)
398
Cenobio
C810
Cabo Verde
El Pagador
Sta. María de Guía
de Gran Canaria
San Juán
El Hormiguero
GC160
Casablanca
San Isidro
14
469
Almagro
Anzofé
La Boticaria
Las Tres Palmas
Frontón
Dragos
Llanos de las Quintanas
El Calabozo
Casa de Aguilar
433
Buenlugar
La Cuesta
GC100
Llano de las Moriscas
Cueva de las Cruces
6,5
San Antonio
Los Paredones
Moya
GC160
GC150
(488)
C810
Los Montañones
Las Tres Cruces
Barranquillo Frío
Lance
(500)
837
Agaete
606
Viento
Vergara
El Junquillo
Firgas
669
17
La Rosa
Verdejo
Santa Cristina
Los Tilos
Casas de Matos
Los Barr
San Fernando
Las Huertecillas
El Chapin
Bascamao
951
Saucillo
El Pedregal
Ermita
San Pedro
Peñón
C814
3
Cazaeta
Vecindad de Entrente
Casas del Camino
Gaideros
Mña Alta
Balneario
Las Madres
968
Los Berrazales
Balneario de Berrazales
Barranco del Laurel
Tablero
Bco del Pinar
Caserón
Zumacal
Gordo
Casas de Tamadaba
1082
Fagajesto
Monagas
Embalse de Los Pérez
San Bartolomé de Fontanales
Valsendero
Zamora
Balcón de Zamora
28
Valleseco
1444
Tamadaba
Los Lugarejos
La Solana
Caldera Pinos de Gáldar
Las Longueras
Lanzarote
Ojeda
4
Casas Las Hoyas
La Coruña
Juncalillo
Madrelagua
3,5
Las Arvejas
El Tablero
GC110
Las Cuevas
Cuevas de Corcho
Presa Ariñez
1335
Artenara
GC110
La Yedra
Brezos
(1250)
Moriscos
Embalse Candelaria
1771
Cruz de Tejeda
Parador Nacional
Ariñez
El Majuelo
1490
Las Lagunetas
Acusa
Guardaya
El Rincón
La Degollada
La Corte
22
5
La Higuerilla
Tejeda
(1049)
C811
Roque Bentayga
Cuevas Caidas
El Chorrillo
1412
Cueva Grande
El Carrizal
El Espinillo
La Solana del Chorrillo
La Culata
1126
Barranco de Siberio
Roque de los Pérez
Hoya del Gramonal
El Toscón
Timagada
1803
1732
Presa de los Hornos
Cruz de
Roque Nublo
1949
Pico de las Nieves
2,5
1919
6
Ayacata
de Sandara
El Juncal
La Culata
Morro de Pajonales
3,5
28
1578
1446
Agualatente
101
C815
105
Cruz de San Antonio

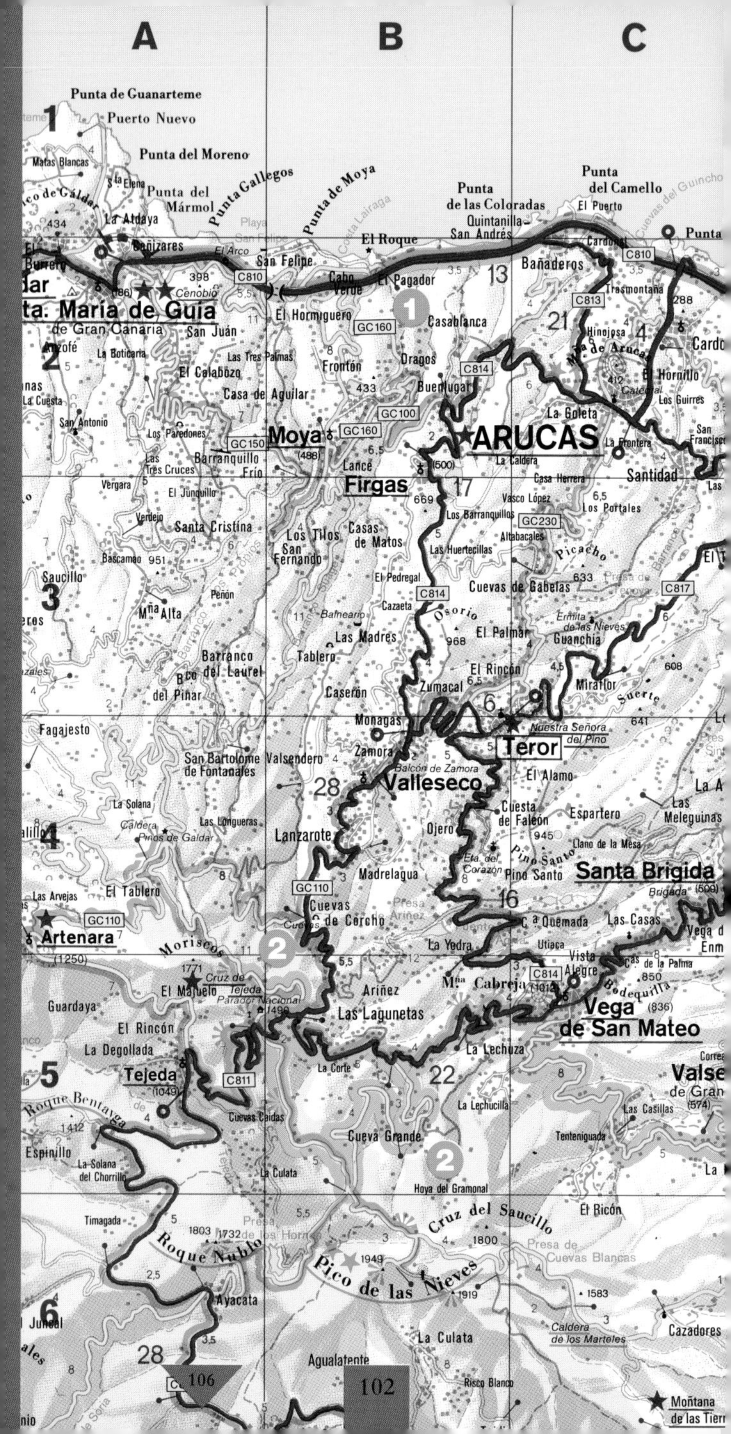
A
B
C
Punta de Guanarteme
Puerto Nuevo
Punta del Moreno
Matas Blancas
Punta del Mármol
Punta Gallegos
Punta de Moya
Punta de las Coloradas
Punta del Camello
El Puerto
Quintanilla-San Andrés
La Atalaya
Cañizares
El Roque
San Felipe
Cabo Verde
El Pagador
Bañaderos
Cardonal
Trasmontaña
C810
C813
Sta. María de Guía
de Gran Canaria
Cenobio
El Hormiguero
GC160
Casablanca
Hinojosa
Mña de Arucas
San Juán
La Boticaria
Las Tres Palmas
Frontón
Dragos
C814
El Hornillo
Catedral
Los Guirres
El Calabozo
Casa de Aguilar
Buenlugar
La Goleta
La Cuesta
San Antonio
GC100
Los Paredones
Moya
ARUCAS
La Frontera
La Caldera
GC150
Barranquillo Frío
Las Tres Cruces
Lance
Firgas
Casa Herrera
Santidad
Vergara
El Junquillo
Vasco López
Los Portales
Los Barranquillos
GC230
Verdejo
Santa Cristina
Los Tilos
Casas de Matos
San Fernando
Las Huertecillas
Altabacales
Picacho
Bascamao
Saucillo
El Pedregal
C814
Cuevas de Gabelas
C817
Peñón
Mña Alta
Balneario
Cazaeta
Osorio
Ermita de las Nieves
Guanchia
Las Madres
El Palmar
Barranco del Laurel
Bco del Pinar
Tablero
El Rincón
Miraflor
Zumacal
Caserón
Suerte
Fagajesto
Monagas
Nuestra Señora del Pino
Teror
San Bartolomé de Fontanales
Valsendero
Zamora
Balcón de Zamora
Valleseco
El Alamo
La Solana
Cuesta de Faleón
Espartero
Las Meleguinas
Caldera Pinos de Galdar
Las Longueras
Lanzarote
Ojero
Llano de la Mesa
Pino Santo
Eta. del Corazón
Santa Brígida
El Tablero
Madrelagua
Brigada
Las Arvejas
GC110
Cuevas de Corcho
Presa Ariñez
Ca Quemada
Las Casas
Artenara
Moriscos
La Yedra
Utiaca
Vista Alegre
Cas de la Palma
Cruz de Tejeda
Parador Nacional
El Majuelo
Mña Cabreja
Ariñez
Las Lagunetas
Bodequilla
Vega de San Mateo
Guardaya
El Rincón
La Degollada
La Lechuza
Tejeda
C811
La Corte
Valsequillo
Roque Bentayga
Cuevas Caídas
La Lechucilla
Las Casillas
Espinillo
La Solana del Chorrillo
Cueva Grande
Tenteniguada
La Culata
Hoya del Gramonal
Timagada
El Ricón
Cruz del Saucillo
Roque Nublo
Presa de los Hornos
Presa de Cuevas Blancas
Pico de las Nieves
Ayacata
Caldera de los Marteles
Cazadores
La Culata
Agualatente
106
Risco Blanco
Montaña de las Tierras

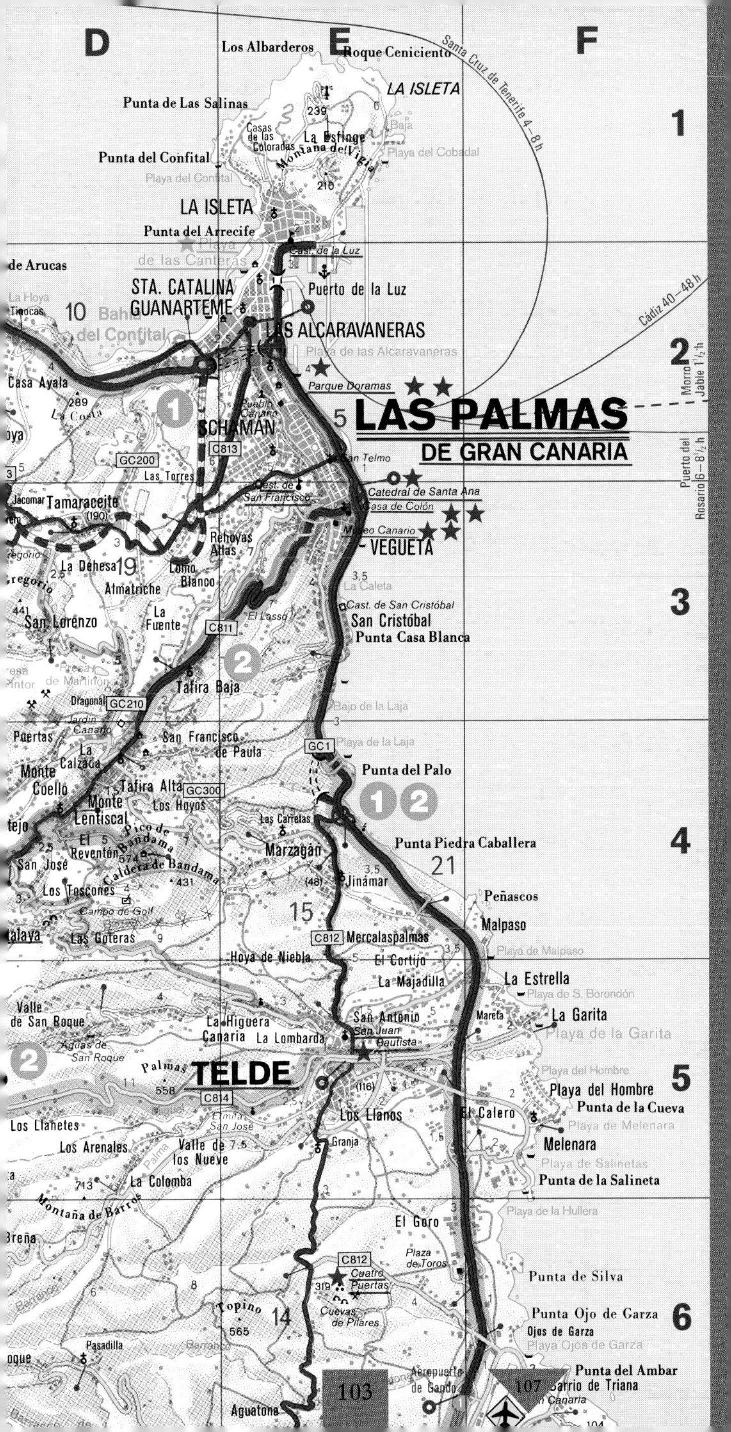
D
E
F
Los Albarderos
Roque Ceniciento
LA ISLETA
Santa Cruz de Tenerife 4–8 h
Punta de Las Salinas
Casas de las Coloradas
La Esfinge
Montaña del Vigía
Playa del Cobadal
Punta del Confital
Playa del Confital
LA ISLETA
Punta del Arrecife
Playa de las Canteras
Cast. de la Luz
de Arucas
STA. CATALINA
GUANARTEME
Puerto de la Luz
Cádiz 40–48 h
La Hoya
Tinocas
Bahía del Confital
LAS ALCARAVANERAS
Playa de las Alcaravaneras
Casa Ayala
Parque Doramas
Morro Jable 1½ h
La Costa
Pueblo Canario
LAS PALMAS
DE GRAN CANARIA
SCHAMAN
C813
GC200
San Telmo
Puerto del Rosario 6–8½ h
Las Torres
Cast. de San Francisco
Catedral de Santa Ana
Casa de Colón
Jacomar
Tamaraceite
Museo Canario
VEGUETA
Rehoyas
Atlas
La Dehesa
Lomo Blanco
Almatriche
La Caleta
Cast. de San Cristóbal
San Lorenzo
La Fuente
El Lasso
San Cristóbal
Punta Casa Blanca
C811
Presa de Martinón
Tafira Baja
Dragonal
GC210
Jardín Canario
Bajo de la Laja
Puertas
San Francisco de Paula
GC1
Playa de la Laja
La Calzada
Punta del Palo
Monte Coello
Tafira Alta
GC300
Monte Lentiscal
Los Hoyos
Pico de Bandama
Las Carretas
Punta Piedra Caballera
El Reventón
Caldera de Bandama
Marzagán
San José
Jinámar
Los Toscones
Campo de Golf
Peñascos
Malpaso
Las Goteras
C812
Mercalaspalmas
Playa de Malpaso
Hoya de Niebla
El Cortijo
La Majadilla
La Estrella
Playa de S. Borondón
Valle de San Roque
La Higuera Canaria
San Antonio
Mareta
La Garita
Playa de la Garita
Aguas de San Roque
La Lombarda
San Juan Bautista
TELDE
Playa del Hombre
C814
Los Llanos
El Calero
Punta de la Cueva
Playa de Melenara
Los Llanetes
Ermita San José
Granja
Melenara
Los Arenales
Valle de los Nueve
Playa de Salinetas
La Colomba
Punta de la Salineta
Montaña de Barros
Playa de la Hullera
El Goro
Breña
Plaza de Toros
C812
Cuatro Puertas
Punta de Silva
Cuevas de Pilares
Topino
Punta Ojo de Garza
Ojos de Garza
Playa Ojos de Garza
Pasadilla
Aeropuerto de Gando
Punta del Ambar
Barrio de Triana
Aguatona
Barranco
103
107
1
2
3
4
5
6

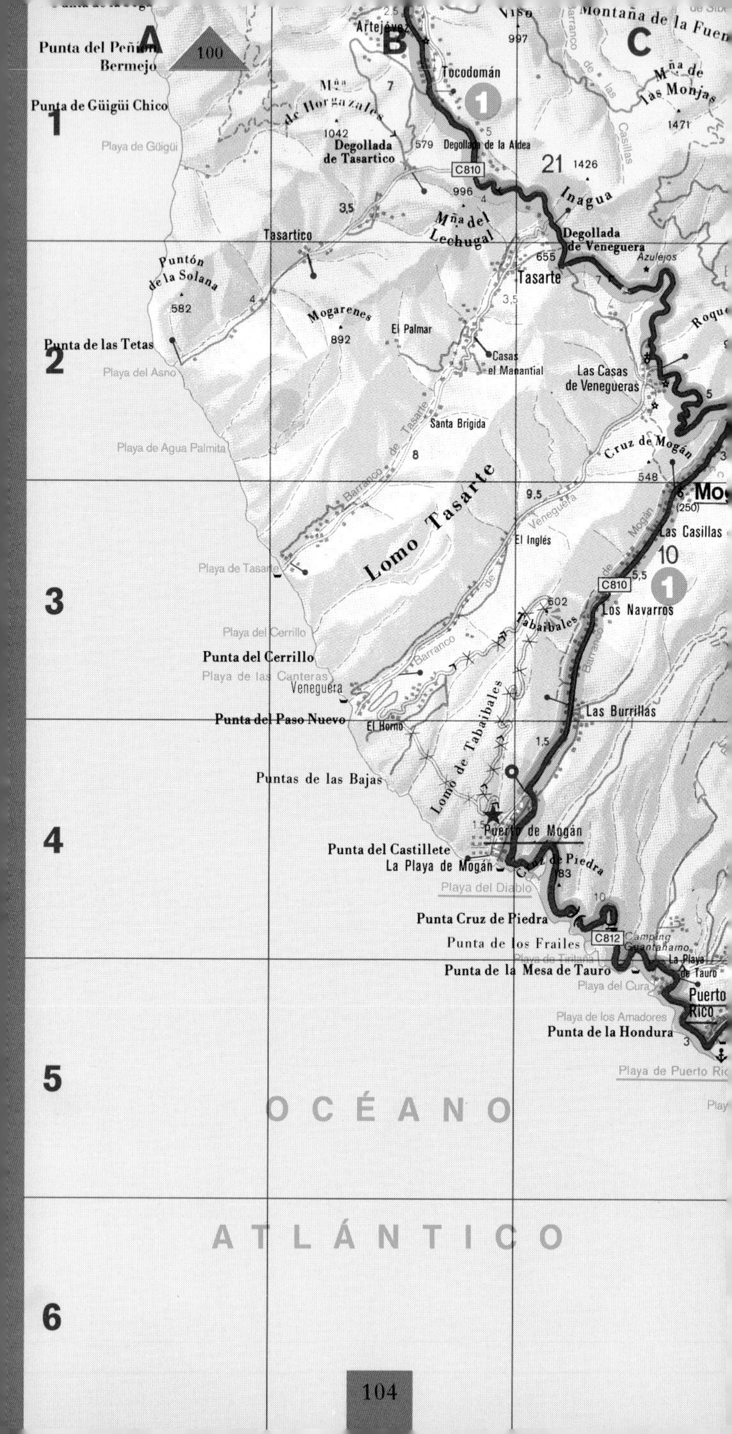

A
B
C
100
1
2
3
4
5
6
Punta del Peñón Bermejo
Punta de Güigüi Chico
Playa de Güigüi
Artejévez
Tocodomán
Viso
997
Montaña de la Fuen
Mña de Horgazales
1042
Degollada de Tasartico
579
Degollada de la Aldea
C810
996
Mña de las Monjas
1471
1426
Inagua
Mña del Lechugal
Tasartico
Degollada de Veneguera
Azulejos
655
Tasarte
Puntón de la Solana
582
Mogarenes
892
El Palmar
Casas el Manantial
Las Casas de Vegueras
Punta de las Tetas
Playa del Asno
Santa Brigida
Barranco de Tasarte
Playa de Agua Palmita
Cruz de Mogán
548
Lomo Tasarte
(250)
Las Casillas
El Inglés
Playa de Tasarte
Los Navarros
602
Tabaibales
Playa del Cerrillo
Punta del Cerrillo
Playa de las Canteras
Veneguera
Las Burrillas
Punta del Paso Nuevo
El Horno
Lomo de Tabaibales
Puntas de las Bajas
Puerto de Mogán
Punta del Castillete
La Playa de Mogán
Cruz de Piedra
Playa del Diablo
Punta Cruz de Piedra
C812
Camping Guantanamo
Punta de los Frailes
Playa de Tiritaña
Punta de la Mesa de Tauro
La Playa de Tauro
Playa del Cura
Puerto Rico
Playa de los Amadores
Punta de la Hondura
Playa de Puerto Rico
OCÉANO
ATLÁNTICO

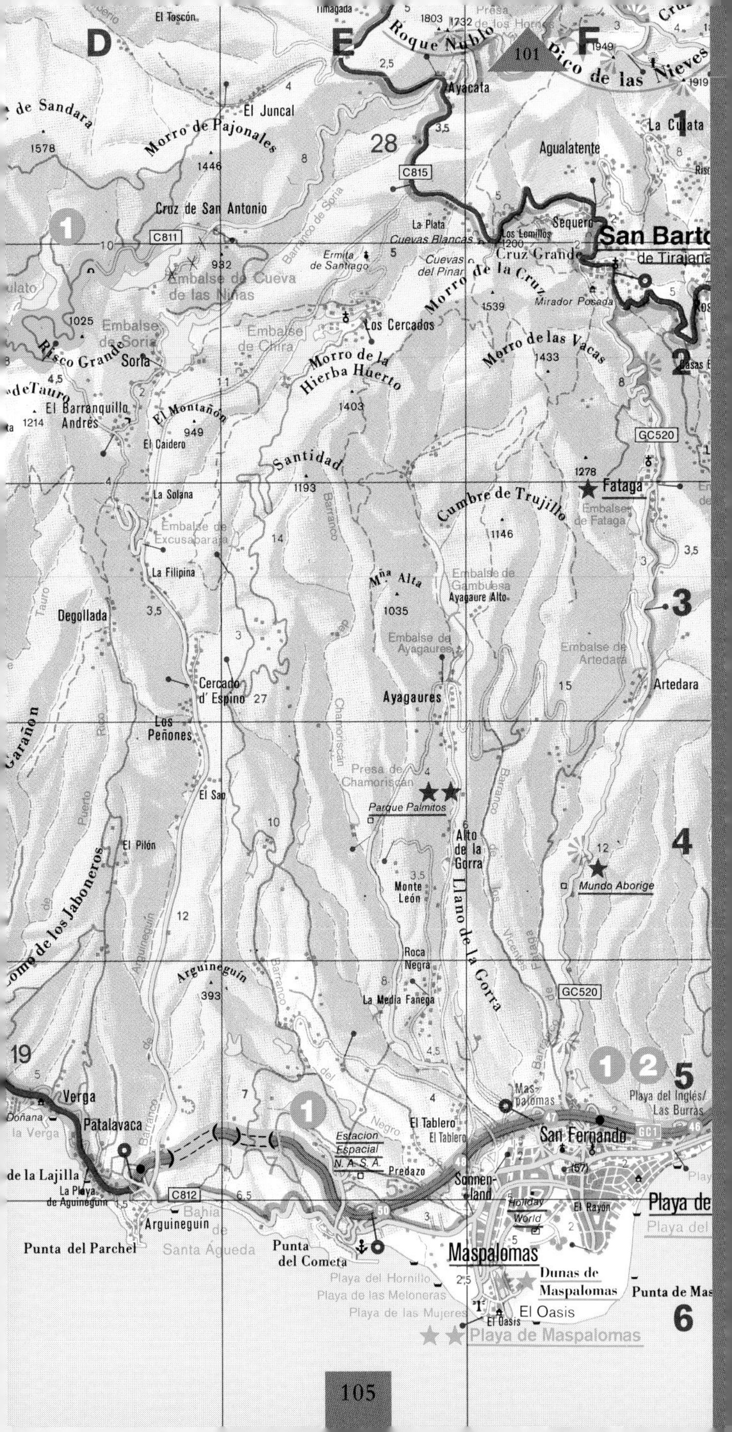

D
E
F
101
28
Roque Nublo
Pico de las Nieves
El Toscón
Ayacata
El Juncal
Morro de Pajonales
1446
1578
Agualatente
La Culata
C815
Cruz de San Antonio
C811
932
Embalse de Cueva de las Niñas
La Plata
Cuevas Blancas
Los Lomillos
1200
Sequero
San Barto
de Tirajana
Cruz Grande
Ermita de Santiago
Cuevas del Pinar
Morro de la Cruz
Mirador Posada
1539
Los Cercados
Embalse de Soria
Embalse de Chira
1025
Risco Grande
Sorìa
Morro de la Hierba Huerto
Morro de las Vacas
1433
1403
El Barranquillo Andrés
1214
El Montañón
949
El Caidero
GC520
Santidad
1193
1278
Fataga
Embalse de Fataga
Cumbre de Trujillo
1146
La Solana
Embalse de Excusabaraja
La Filipina
Mña Alta
1035
Embalse de Gambuesa
Ayagaure Alto
Degollada
Embalse de Ayagaures
Embalse de Artedara
Artedara
Cercado d' Espino
27
Ayagaures
Los Peñones
Presa de Chamoriscán
Parque Palmitos
El Sao
Alto de la Gorra
Mundo Aborige
El Pilón
Monte León
Llano de la Gorra
Lomo de los Jaboneros
Roca Negra
Arguineguín
393
La Media Fanega
GC520
19
Verga
Doñana
la Verga
Patalavaca
Estacion Espacial N. A. S. A.
Predazo
El Tablero
Mas-palomas
San Fernando
Playa del Inglés/ Las Burras
GC1
de la Lajilla
La Playa de Aguineguín
C812
Bahía de Santa Águeda
Arguineguín
Sonnen-land
Holiday World
El Rayon
Playa de
Punta del Parchel
Punta del Cometa
Maspalomas
Playa del Hornillo
Playa de las Meloneras
Playa de las Mujeres
Dunas de Maspalomas
Punta de Mas
El Oasis
Playa de Maspalomas
1
2
3
4
5
6

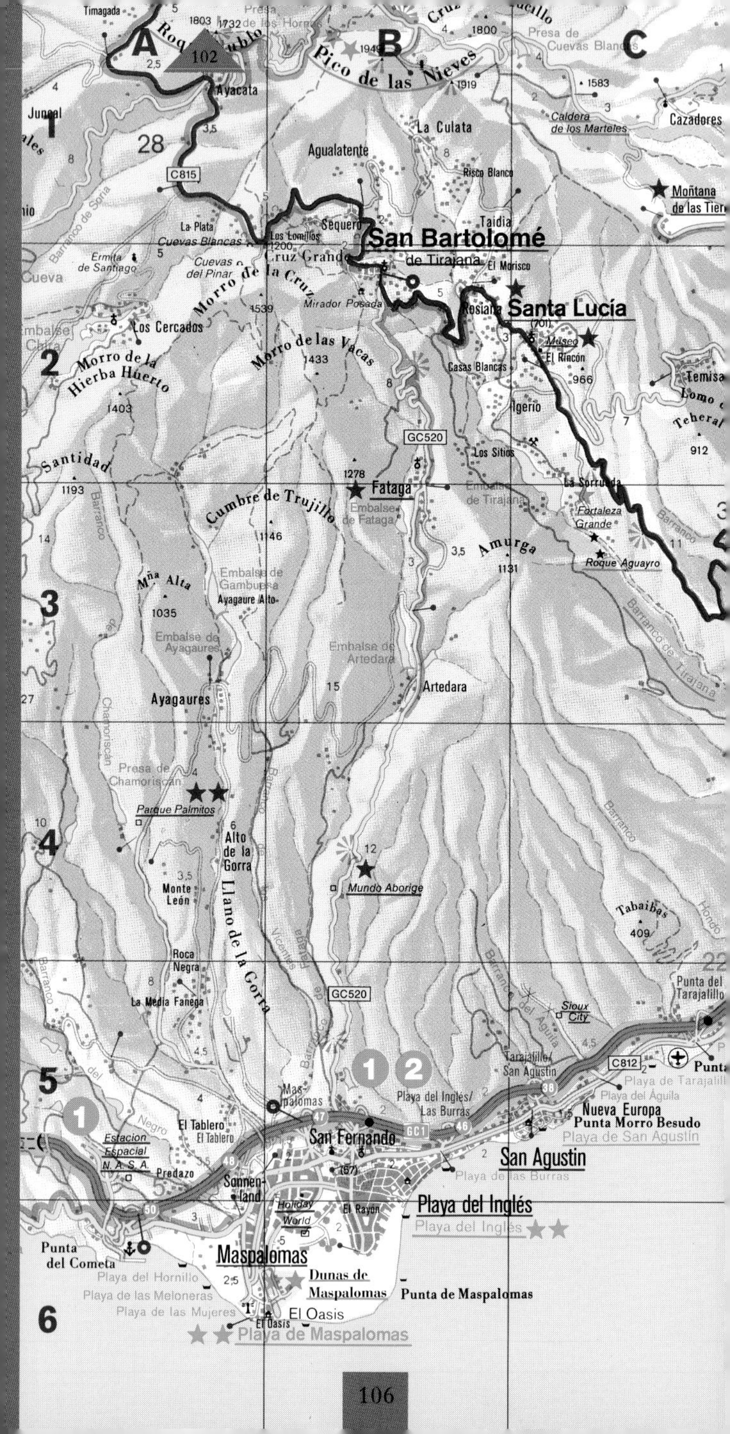
A
B
C
1
2
3
4
5
6
Timagada
Roque Nublo
Presa de los Hornos
Pico de las Nieves
Presa de Cuevas Blancas
102
Ayacata
Juncal
28
C815
Caldera de los Marteles
Cazadores
La Culata
Agualatente
Risco Blanco
Moñtana de las Tierras
Taidia
Sequero
Los Lomillos
La Plata
Cuevas Blancas
San Bartolomé
de Tirajana
El Morisco
Cruz Grande
Ermita de Santiago
Cuevas del Pinar
Morro de la Cruz
Mirador Posada
Rosiana
Santa Lucía
Los Cercados
Museo
El Rincón
Morro de las Vacas
Casas Blancas
Temisas
Morro de la Hierba Huerto
Lomo
Teheral
Ingerio
GC520
Los Sitios
Santidad
Fataga
Embalse de Fataga
Embalse de Tirajana
La Sorrueda
Fortaleza Grande
Roque Aguayro
Cumbre de Trujillo
Amurga
Mña Alta
Embalse de Gambuesa
Ayagaure Alto
Embalse de Ayagaures
Embalse de Artedara
Barranco de Tirajana
Artedara
Ayagaures
Presa de Chamoriscán
Parque Palmitos
Alto de la Gorra
Monte León
Mundo Aborige
Llano de la Gorra
Tabaibas
Roca Negra
La Media Fanega
Sioux City
Punta del Tarajalillo
Tarajalillo/ San Agustín
C812
Playa de Tarajalillo
Playa del Águila
Mas-palomas
Playa del Inglés/ Las Burras
Nueva Europa
Punta Morro Besudo
El Tablero
San Fernando
GC1
Playa de San Agustín
Estacion Espacial N.A.S.A.
Predazo
San Agustin
Playa de las Burras
Sonnen-land
Holiday World
El Rayón
Playa del Inglés
Punta del Cometa
Maspalomas
Playa del Hornillo
Dunas de Maspalomas
Playa de las Meloneras
Punta de Maspalomas
Playa de las Mujeres
El Oasis
Playa de Maspalomas

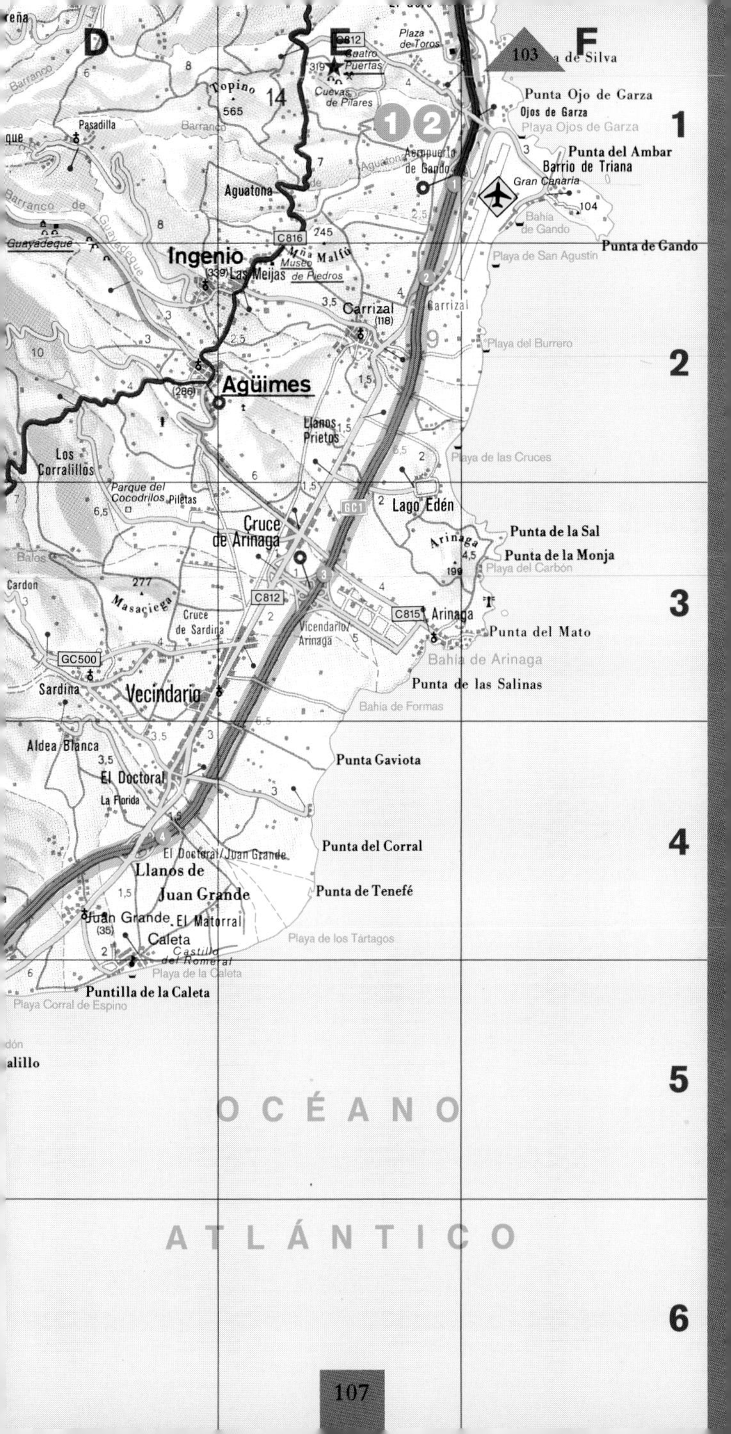
D
E
F
103
a de Silva
Plaza de Toros
C812
Cuatro Puertas
Cuevas de Pilares
Topino
565
14
Pasadilla
Barranco
Punta Ojo de Garza
Ojos de Garza
Playa Ojos de Garza
Aeropuerto de Gando
Punta del Ambar
Barrio de Triana
Gran Canaria
104
Bahía de Gando
Punta de Gando
Aguatona
Guayadeque
245
C816
Ingenio
Las Meijas
Museo de Piedros
Malfú
Playa de San Agustín
Carrizal
Playa del Burrero
Agüimes
Llanos Prietos
Los Corralillos
Playa de las Cruces
Parque del Cocodrilos
Piletas
Lago Edén
Cruce de Arinaga
Punta de la Sal
Punta de la Monja
Playa del Carbón
Balos
Cardon
Masaciega
C812
Cruce de Sardina
C815
Arinaga
Vicendario/Arinaga
Punta del Mato
Bahía de Arinaga
GC500
Sardina
Vecindario
Punta de las Salinas
Bahía de Formas
Aldea Blanca
Punta Gaviota
El Doctoral
La Florida
Punta del Corral
El Doctoral/Juan Grande
Llanos de Juan Grande
Punta de Tenefé
Juan Grande
El Matorral
Caleta
Castillo del Romeral
Playa de los Tártagos
Playa de la Caleta
Puntilla de la Caleta
Playa Corral de Espino
GC1
OCÉANO
ATLÁNTICO
1
2
3
4
5
6

Islas Canarias
(España)

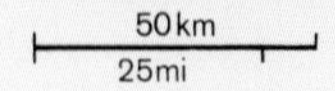

O C É A N O A

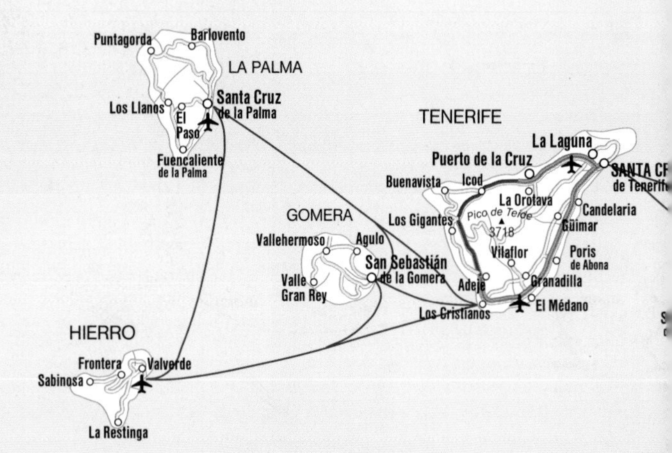